Snake River Country

Flies and Waters

Bruce Staples

Frank Amato Publications
Portland, Oregon

Bruce Staples, a native New Englander, has lived in eastern Idaho since the mid 1960s. He started fly fishing in 1970 and was introduced to fly tying a few years later. He has fly fished most of the waters in eastern Idaho, southwestern Montana, and western Wyoming. His main interests in fly tying are the creation of effective patterns and the modification of traditional ones to improve their effectiveness. His numerous articles have appeared in *American Angler and Fly Tyer* and *Fly Fisher* magazines. He has participated as a demonstrating tier in several International Conclaves of the Federation of Fly Fishers (FFF) and is a member of the FFF and the Dutch-American Association of Fly Tyers (DAAFT). He instructs all levels of fly tying, ties commercially, writes a monthly fly fishing column for the *Idaho Falls Post Register,* and maintains an interest in the art and history of fly tying. He is a long time member of the Upper Snake River Chapter of Trout Unlimited in Idaho Falls and of the Upper Snake River Fly Fishers of Rexburg.

Dennis Swanson

Copyright 1991 • Bruce Staples
Illustrators: Gerry Arrington & Barry Staples
Book Design: Joyce Herbst • Typesetting: Charlie Clifford
Softbound ISBN: 1-878175-08-4 • Hardbound ISBN: 1-878175-09-2

Front Cover: *John Haugh fishing Henry's Fork.* Frank Amato

10 9 8 7 6 5 4 3 2

Frank Amato Publications
P.O. Box 82112, Portland, OR 97282
(503) 653-8108 • FAX: (503) 653-2766
Printed in Hong Kong

ACKNOWLEDGEMENTS

There is a "down home" saying that applies to almost any task that a person completes. It goes: "I take my cream from many cows, but I make my own butter." In every sense this allegory applies to the composition of this book because there have been many generous contributors. Several individuals supplied photographs, and recognition is given at the end of each caption. At the end of this book I recognize the tiers who contributed flies to be photographed and discussed. They also supplied information on the use and history of the flies, and I thank each of them for their contributions.

There are others, however, who supplied information I needed for this task. To Charles "Chip" Corsi, Dick Scully, Steve Elle, and Larry Labolle of the Idaho Department of Fish and Game I owe thanks for information on the history and goals of cold water fisheries management in eastern Idaho. I had many enjoyable conversations about eastern Idaho fisheries with Paul Jeppson of Rigby, the former District 6 fisheries manager and biologist who worked out of the Idaho Falls Office. I thank Paul for the information he shared with me.

Jim and Jimmy Gabettas, the father and son outdoorsmen who operate the quality fly fishing shops (All Seasons Angler in Idaho Falls and Pocatello), deserve thanks for the information they graciously provided about tiers, flies, and area waters.

Thanks also goes to Dr. Jim McCue, Dr. Kenneth Krell, Dennis Bitton, Vince Esparza, Harold Roberts of Idaho Falls, Mrs. Paul Clements of Ririe, Ralph Moon of Chester, Spence Warner of Swan Valley , Elton Bybee of Pocatello, Paul Bowen of Rexburg, Jerry Berg of Soda Springs, Mike McCoy of Bothell, Washington, and Bear McKinney of Jackson, Wyoming for providing me with important material. I recognize Darrel Lindsay of Soda Springs, George Biggs of Jerome, Dee Vissing of Idaho Falls, Ardell Jeppsen of Benjamin, Utah and Laurn and Elgarda Ashliman of Rexburg for providing specific information about flies they conceived.

My fly tying experience goes back to the early 1970s. Three people had much influence on my early days in this activity, and I thank them now for their inspiration and encouragement. They are Pat and Sig Barnes and the late Stan Yamamura. Later I became acquainted with Charlie Brooks. In this brief acquaintance Charlie shared fly fishing information with me that has proven to be invaluable. I also owe thanks to Gary Borger, who provided suggestions concerning the manuscript of this book, and to Jenni Casper and my wife, Carol, who prepared it. Gerry Arrington and my son Barry contributed art work.

Bing and Dorothy Lempke are special to all of us who enjoy fly fishing. Many evenings, before Bing passed away, they welcomed me into their home in Idaho Falls where we discussed all aspects of fly fishing. I consider these visits a privilege, and I thank Bing and Dorothy because our discussions influenced the content of this book. Many of us who have an interest in fly fishing have gone to Bing with questions and ideas. The results of conversations were always constructive and informative. Bing's influence also extended to those who never had the pleasure of meeting him. His contributions to understanding trout behavior, aquatic entomology, and creations of unique fly tying techniques are gifts to all of us.

In the 1960's and 1970's the late Stan Yamamura was eastern Idaho's premier commercial tier. He was also a fly designer of national reputation. Creations such as his Stan's Hopper and Stan's Willow Fly are still local favorites. Many area tiers have benefited from Stan's techniques and creativity. Bruce Staples

CONTENTS

PART I

PART II

The author casting a fly to visible trout. Frank Amato

INTRODUCTION

Clearly this is a regional book. Much of its content, however, can be applied to other areas because eastern Idaho waters are almost unequalled in variety. Likewise, the diversity of flies that are useful here is almost unequalled, and thus one can find patterns that will be effective (under similar circumstances) in other areas.

This book is also descriptive—I have divided it into two main sections, one overviewing the waters and another discussing popular flies. This approach, I believe, gives the contemplative fly fisher grist for putting together his own fishing experience without burdening him too much with mine.

The overview of area waters is divided into three separate sections—trunk streams, highland drainages, and sinks drainages—because each has its own specific characteristics. Each could be a subject of individual attention, but I'll leave that to someone else. You will find that I have omitted descriptions of certain waters. That is because I have not fished all the water available in the area. To do so comprehensibly would take an enjoyable lifetime of fishing.

The only part of eastern Idaho that has been subjected to systematic attention is the Island Park area of the Henry's Fork drainage. Several books containing great detail on the fishing in this area are available. If one wishes to develop a fishing strategy for this area, however, I must recommend reading Charlie Brook's spellbinding book *The Henry's Fork*. It is simply the best, but it is not Charlie's only work which applies to this area. Add to this gift to all fishermen the information available in his books *Larger Trout for Western Fishermen*, and *Fishing Yellowstone Waters*, along with Bill Schiess' *Fishing Henry's Lake*, and numerous magazine articles and videos describing the area and you will have many hours of material to form an approach to fishing the Island Park waters.

The flies described in the following pages are by no means the only locally effective patterns, but they are the most popular. Here you will find old standbys in widespread use. You will also find patterns created here, in eastern Idaho, and patterns created in other places. Many of these flies have served as the basis of modification by creative fly tiers, resident and non-resident alike. I have discussed many of these variations but, perhaps unjustly, not every one.

There is a distasteful practice in progress today. Recognition hungry fly tiers opportunistically seek out patterns conceived by others in relatively obscure locations. When original or effective patterns are found these opportunists go to other surroundings to proclaim them as their own creations. This practice is at least misrepresentation and at most outright theft. I object to this practice, and in the past have published articles giving credit to local tiers who have had patterns stolen. I continue this practice of giving credit in this book, while also revealing the rich fly tying tradition evolving in eastern Idaho. Fly patterns that originated outside our area but have proven effective here and therefore are popular are also discussed. Thus, I also give credit to the creators of these patterns or to those linked to them in a constructive manner. Rest assured that if one were to use only the flies described here, he or she would surely have successful fishing in eastern Idaho waters. But realize that there are other flies that are also effective if presented equally well.

Consider this book to be an attempt to shed light on an area that has as much to offer as the more storied areas adjacent to it. Also be aware that there is trouble in the form of continuing habitat degradation in this fly fishing paradise. Thus, part of the purpose of this book is to illustrate what we have to lose and to arouse the reader to fight to preserve what is left.

Scenery is a special bonus for Henry's Fork anglers in Harriman State Park. Formerly known as the Railroad Ranch, the Park's waters and surroundings are a national treasure. Few waters have been heralded in print as much as the Henry's Fork in Harriman State Park, and the acclaim is well deserved. There are potential threats to future quality of this reach from an upstream hydro-project being installed in Island Park Dam and from timbering activities in surrounding forests. Awareness of the economic value of the Henry's Fork fishery to eastern Idaho, however, is increasing such that many organizations work to protect its quality. Mike Lawson

PART I

SNAKE RIVER COUNTRY

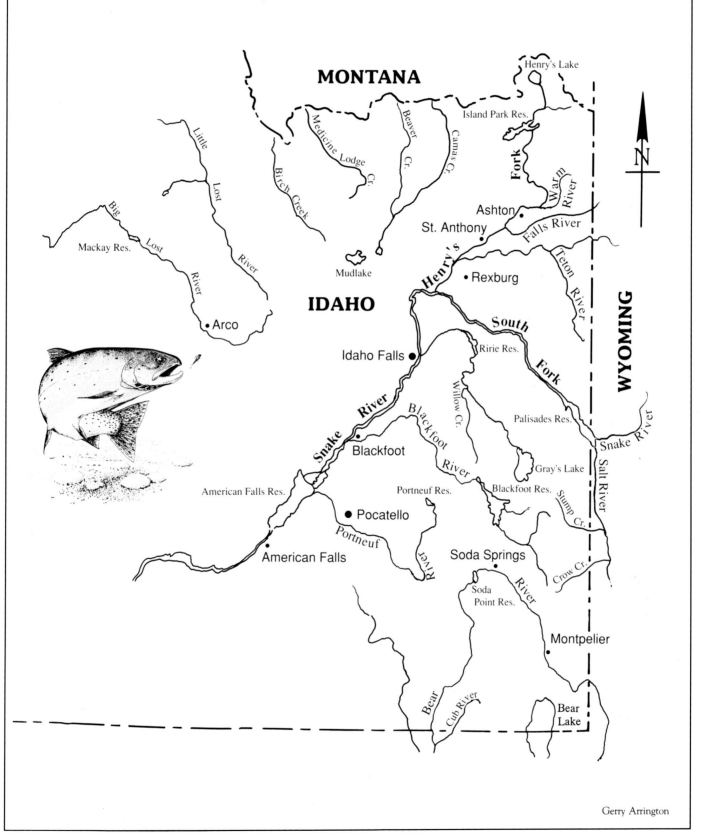

Gerry Arrington

ABOUT THE WATERS

Up to the early nineteenth century the Intermountain Region, of which most of eastern Idaho is a part, held vast, unspoiled cold water fisheries in which various strains of cutthroat trout were a major component. Only the relatively sparse population of Native Americans used this trout population for subsistence without inflicting any serious negative effects on it. This use was adopted by the first white and black men who came here as missionaries or to hunt, trap, or explore in the first few decades of the nineteenth century. Their journals contain many descriptions of catching "salmon trout" by various means to provide table fare. But this use resulted in very little population loss or habitat alteration in the lakes and streams of the area. Thus the vast populations of trout hosted in many of these waters remained intact up to the mid nineteenth century—a mere 150 years ago.

Settlement of the area and use of lands adjacent to waters for agricultural and stock raising purposes initiated the degradation of lakes and streams resulting in the decline of cold water fisheries. In the first few decades after the mid nineteenth century there was little overall effect on trout populations. But in specific locales populations were being seriously impacted by diversion of water for agriculture, and by heavy livestock usage. Such was happening in central Utah where a population of Bonneville cutthroat trout (containing individuals of massive size) in Utah Lake was becoming

Trumpeter swans are seen on many eastern Idaho waters. Important populations frequent the waters around the Henry's Fork, Gray's Lake, Bear Lake, Market Lake, Blackfoot Reservoir and the Snake River proper. Ken Retallic

An indicator of midsummer, the Indian paint brush is common in the valleys and foothills. Marv Hoyt

extinct, and also in southern Utah where a healthy cutthroat trout population in the Sevier River system was disappearing.

In eastern Idaho isolated livestock and agricultural activities started in the 1840s. Widespread occupation started in the 1860s with the dispersion of peoples to the Snake River Plain and to the highlands in present day Franklin, Oneida, Caribou and Bear Lake counties. It was a harsh life for these pioneers, and in order to survive, natural resources had to be utilized to the fullest extent. By the 1870s impacts on the cold water fisheries had begun. Vast herds of cattle and sheep ranged along the Lander, Oregon, and California trails, and up the South Fork of the Snake River causing bank erosion and riparian zone destruction, providing a growing threat to the quality of lakes and streams. On the Snake River Plain more and more water was being diverted from streams for agriculture resulting in the loss of both habitat and fish. Settlement of Teton Valley, the Lost River valleys, and the Swan and Grand valleys of the South Fork of the Snake River was next. Last came settlement of more remote areas away from the Snake River Plain.

Activities involving livestock and agriculture degraded fisheries in many of these locations. By the turn of the century the overall quality of the fisheries in most of the valleys had been significantly altered. Next, timbering and mining had negative effects, particularly along headwater streams. But the various fisheries still held huge numbers of trout. Shortly after the turn of the century agricultural needs for surface water increased to the point that another demand was made on area streams—dams to store water for irrigation. The Blackfoot River Reservoir was among the first. It was soon followed by Mackay Reservoir on Big Lost River, Henry's Lake Dam, American Falls Reservoir on the Snake River, Chesterfield Reservoir on the Portneuf River, and Island Park Reservoir on the Henry's Fork. Dams to provide hydropower to growing populations were also built including Ashton Dam on the lower Henry's Fork, Felt Dam in Teton Canyon, Soda Point, Grace and Oneida dams on the Bear River, and dams on the Snake River to serve Idaho Falls. Later more dams were constructed to store water, provide hydropower, or for flood control. These included Palisades Dam on the South Fork of the Snake River, Ririe Dam on lower Willow Creek, the ill-fated dam on the Teton River, and Gem State Dam on the Snake River below Idaho Falls. All these dams have not had entirely negative impacts on the streams hosting them; however, each has forever changed the stream on which it was built—and more dams are planned for eastern Idaho's rivers.

Impacts from agriculture, livestock, mining, hydropower, and timbering have left us with a remnant of the original overall fisheries quality and quantity in eastern Idaho. Thus, within this area one can also find all degrees of quality from pristine to, regrettably, complete despoliation. In certain cases this range of conditions can be found within one stream. In area waters one will still find an unequalled complement of salmonids including the native cutthroat trout and whitefish along with exotic brook trout, brown trout and rainbow trout. Each trout species is widespread and all grow to trophy size. Limited populations of exotic golden trout, mackinaw, grayling and an isolated population of native bull trout can also be found. Anadromous fish are missing—barred from this area, at least in historic times, by Shoshone Falls on the Snake River just upstream of Twin Falls in south central Idaho.

The remnant cold water fishery in eastern Idaho is still one of the best on the North American continent. What has happened here to degrade our fishery appears to be the norm considering the encroachment of civilization; fisheries in other areas have even been more degraded than eastern Idaho. But we now have technology and management concepts to reverse this degradation. We also are beginning to realize what we have lost by despoiling this valuable natural resource of high quality waters. Thus advocate groups interested in preserving what is left and, yes, even restoring some of the former quality to the fisheries through use of this technology and management are gaining in strength. Still one must ask if we have gone too far in our degradation. Let us hope not, and let us all strive to preserve what is left.

TRUNK STREAMS

Standing on the most southerly and not too lofty Menan Butte one gets a perspective of the trunk stream system of eastern Idaho. Facing east, the South Fork of the Snake River in a verdant fringe is seen flowing almost straight across the plain from its canyon between the Big Hole and Caribou ranges. From its course irrigation canals radiate like branches from the trunk of a tree. On the north horizon one sees Big Bend Ridge through which the Henry's Fork cuts after it gathers its sources in the Island Park area. To the northeast the Henry's Fork, tapped by irrigation canals, turns in slow arcs through the plain to its confluence with the South Fork, almost at one's feet. To the native east Idahoan this is the start of the Snake River. Facing south one sees it flow west around the butte then arc southwesterly into the blue haze of the plain. On it flows through the monotonous flats accepting first the remnants of Willow Creek then those of the Blackfoot River. On through the degraded cottonwood forest above the broad expanse of American Falls Reservoir it courses. Here it pauses and takes in the Portneuf River and numerous spring creeks before plunging more westerly to exit eastern Idaho. For more than a century the trunk streams have supplied life-blood water to agricultural activities, industries, and towns in the Snake River Plain. These activities in turn have had a profound influence on the trunk streams and their trout populations as we shall see in the following discussion.

Perhaps native to some eastern Idaho waters in days gone by, grayling are planted mainly in high mountain lakes by the Idaho Department of Fish and Game. One exception to this is the planted population in Horseshoe Lake east of Ashton and off Cave Falls road. Jimmy Gabettas

Snake River

From Lake Walcott upstream to American Falls Dam the Snake River is confined to a spectacular canyon. This is big water best fished from a boat, but just below American Falls Dam (and at a few locations in the canyon) one can reach the water to fish streamers or nymphs year-round and always have a chance of fooling a large trout. The great expanse of American Falls Reservoir, created in 1927, offers little to the fly fisher not using a boat. Above the impoundment the mainstream Snake flows through a riparian zone and offers more as a cold water fishery.

In this reach the river is mainly a large riffle and run stream with holes formed by fissures and voids in the lava bed rock. No comprehensive history of fishing the Snake River exists, nor of its adjacent waters in the valley floor. However, from the glimpses we have into fishing in the last century we can deduce that better conditions existed. Regrettably, the development of eastern Idaho has resulted in the siltation, pollution and periodic dewatering of this reach up to the confluence of the South Fork and Henry's Fork. Still, good fishing in season can be found, mostly by boat fishing,

but also at certain locations where entry is on public land or where private owners will grant passage.

The best fishing in the reach just above American Falls Reservoir is not necessarily on the river but in adjacent spring creeks, which in some cases flow for miles to contribute large volumes of water to the river or the reservoir. A few of these, such as Danielson Creek, which hosts Springfield Reservoir, and McTucker Creek are west of the river. Most are east of it on the Fort Hall Indian Reservation. They can be fished by obtaining a reservation permit and are subject to tribal regulations. Spring Creek, with a base flow of 650 cubic feet per second at its source below Ferry Butte, is the major stream. For nearly 20 miles it follows a convoluted course to American Falls Reservoir. Other spring creeks of note are Big Jimmy Creek, Clear Creek, and Kinney Creek. Cutthroat, rainbow and a few brown trout sometimes reach enormous sizes in these creeks. The main degradation to the creeks is overgrazing by domestic cattle, but successful efforts are being made to reverse resultant bank erosion and to restore damag-

At least in historical times rainbow trout were not native to the Snake River Country above Shoshone Falls in south central Idaho. After introduction decades ago they have flourished. The spring creeks and impoundments above American Falls Reservoir produce many trophies like this, but large rainbows can be found throughout Snake River Country. Bas Verschoor.

ed riparian zones. In season, caddisfly, damselfly, mayfly and midge emergences occur on the spring creeks triggering feeding sessions by resident trout that provide challenging fishing. Many accomplished fly fishers claim that the profusion of aquatic insects in these spring creeks nearly matches that found in Henry's Fork in the Island Park area. Access to spring creeks on Fort Hall Indian Reservation is obtained by travelling west from U.S. Highway 91 to the Fort Hall Bottoms on either Sheepskin Road (which follows portions of the original Oregon Trail) or on Broncho Road. Large streamer, nymph and leach patterns usually take the best fish from small impoundments (such as Springfield Reservoir west of the river), the Snake River, and the spring creeks.

In this reach, as one courses upstream along the Snake, channel alterations are passed, but it is numerous irrigation diversions that degrade the river most. Seasonally they take great quantities of water and return only a polluted token. As is the case with other trunk steams, quantities of fingerling and fry are lost from the river into these canals. Below and above the city of Idaho Falls, hydropower dams interrupt autumn runs of spawning brown trout and spring runs of spawning rainbows. Suitable spawning habitat remains in the river, but future dams planned for Idaho Falls and other towns adjacent to the river could have negative impacts on what spawning habitat remains.

Traditionally the river in this reach is open to fishing year-

Browns that dwarf even this ten-pound bruiser inhabit the lower Henry's Fork, the South Fork of the Snake River and the Snake River proper. Brown trout were introduced to eastern Idaho waters decades ago, and now the trunk streams and several other drainages hold browns ranging to trophy size. Bruce Staples

round, and during winter provides respite for home-bound anglers. In all, the river can provide a good day's fishing before runoff or in the low waters of late autumn or early winter. Remnant emergences of aquatic insects occur and can provide some sport, but again it is the concentration of fish in deeper runs and pools that offers the best chances to those fishing deep with streamers or nymphs.

The Snake River below American Falls Dam is eastern Idaho's largest river. With the exception of the sinks drainage and the Bear River drainage all other waters have gathered above here. Rattlesnake Island is seven miles below American Falls Dam. Boating is the best approach to fishing these waters. Jimmy Gabettas

THE HENRY'S FORK

To most east Idahoans the smaller or westerly fork of the Snake River below Menan Buttes is known as the North Fork, but formally it is the Henry's Fork of the Snake River. Upstream, to the area of the North Fork of the Teton River, it has undergone recent and devastating degradation by the flood resulting from the Saturday June 5, 1976 failure of Teton Dam. Time is repairing the damage, and once again it produces catches of brown, cutthroat and rainbow trout if one uses the same fishing strategy as on the main Snake River. Superficially the section of the Henry's Fork, from its confluence upstream to the area of the North Fork of the Teton River, resembles the mainstream Snake just above

Above the confluence with the North Fork of the Teton River the quality of Henry's Fork improves noticeably up to Chester Dam (location of a major irrigation diversion). In this reach good aquatic insect populations are present, but habitat conditions are compromised somewhat because of siltation from Falls River runoff. The river is open to fishing year-round and about the only time it is not fishable is during hard winter freezes and when springtime runoff from Falls River (entering just above the Chester Dam) muddies it.

Above the Falls River confluence is where the Henry's Fork of story and fame really begins. Massive populations of giant

This bright nineteen-inch brown took a streamer in Ashton Reservoir on the Lower Henry's Fork. Browns were introduced only a few decades ago in the lower river and reservoir. They inhabit the river upstream into Cardiac Canyon below Mesa Falls and now provide sport for anglers using bait, flies and lures. Bruce Staples

American Falls Reservoir. Here also the river meanders through a degraded riparian zone, and a number of spring streams feed it, mainly from the east. Most of these springs are on private land, and owner permission to fish will be granted in some cases. Generally these springs suffer from degradation brought on by years of siltation from livestock usage, diversion for agricultural purposes, and effects from the Teton Dam break. Still, good fish can be found in some of these spring fed streams, and obtaining permission to fish them in season is worth the effort. Good populations of aquatic insects are present, and nymph, emerger and adult imitations along with streamers can gain the interest of resident trout.

stoneflies, not affected by siltation from high country runoff or irrigation diversions, thrive in this free flowing seven mile stretch. One also finds thick caddis emergences in springtime and early summer, and nearly year-round midge and varied mayfly hatches. Many of the aquatic insect species present in the Box Canyon to Riverside reach in Island Park are also found in these quality waters. Little siltation enters because of ancient Ashton Dam, and there is only minor agricultural runoff below it. This combination along with an easy gradient, good cover and suitable spawning areas suggest that a superior fishery should be present. It is, however, the heavy pressure to fill bag limits by fly, lure and bait

The Henry's Fork just downstream of the ancient Ashton Dam is as rich as any river in terms of insect life. It holds a trout population that has endured a century of subsistence fishing. Only remnant numbers of truly large trout remain in the healthy population. Restrictive regulations on this reach would surely result in numbers of large trout that would rival those found in the Last Chance-Harriman State Park reach in Island Park. Bruce Staples

fishers that prevents this fabulously productive reach from being the equal of the Box Canyon to Riverside reach, at least with respect to large fish. Despite this pressure a few large rainbow and brown trout inhabit this reach, and one never knows when a deeply fished streamer, stonefly nymph, or a large floating pattern fished during the stonefly emergence or terrestrial season will entice a strike from one of these lunkers.

Henry's Fork is best fished by boat above Ashton Reservoir to just below Warm River. The presence of enormous brown trout in the Ashton Reservoir to Warm River reach attracts many fly fishers. Decades ago rainbow trout were introduced into this reach, and as in Henry's Fork in general, have hybridized over the years with the native cutthroat trout. Today pure native cutthroat are not common. Brown trout were first introduced into this reach through canal salvage operations along the South Fork of the

Snake River in the 1960s by Idaho Department of Fish and Game. In the 1970s the Department's studies revealed a depletion of cutthroat-rainbow hybrid trout from the reach because of heavy fishing pressure. Then quantities of brown trout fingerlings were introduced each spring just after runoff from 1980-1982 in a cooperative effort by the Idaho Department of Fish and Game, members of the Upper Snake River Chapter of Trout Unlimited (Idaho Falls), and also with help from members of the Upper Snake River Fly Fishers of Rexburg. In this undertaking eyed brown trout eggs were purchased with funds raised by the Chapter at the first of each year. Incubation of the eggs to fingerling size was done in the Ashton Hatchery.

After spring runoff the fingerling browns were released at various sites in the upper part of the reach: in the Bear Gulch area, in Robinson Creek, and upstream in Warm River to the old hat-

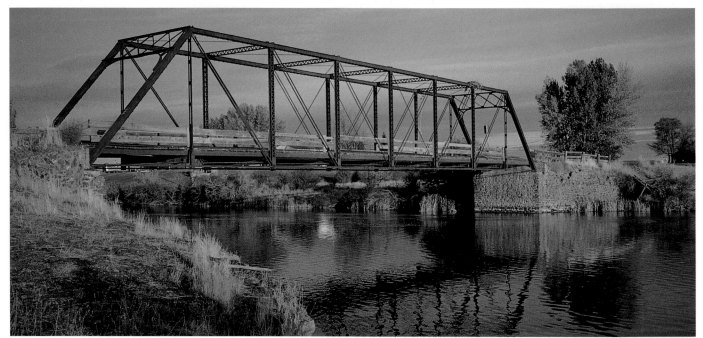

chery at Warm River Spring. This action has resulted in an established brown trout population with immense individuals occasionally being caught. The brown trout supplement the more easily depleted rainbow and cutthroat-rainbow hybrids, all of which provide sport mainly for boat fishermen using adult and nymph stonefly imitations and large streamers or hopper patterns. The presence of brown trout is not only making this reach a new destination for fly fishers seeking challenging angling, but is also taking angling pressure off other streams in eastern Idaho.

"See you at the Fun Farm Bridge!" This well-known landmark on the Henry's Fork between the towns of Chester and Saint Anthony is a long-time jumping off point for float fishers and walk-in anglers alike. The Fun Farm is a resort, now renamed Teton View, and this old iron bridge is one of the few of its type remaining in eastern Idaho. Bruce Staples

Sunset on the lower Henry's Fork. The Snake River Plain provides a big sky panorama that makes this end of the day event the best that nature offers. Paul Bowen

ISLAND PARK

With respect to geomorphology the Island Park area is a collapsed caldera with a southern rim, known as Big Bend Ridge, running in an arc from the Centennial Range on the west to the Madison Plateau on the east. The 20 mile long trench that the Henry's Fork cuts through the east edge of the caldera is known unofficially as Cardiac Canyon. In this magnificent and isolated gorge the Henry's Fork is similar to what it was 200 years ago. Only a few roads penetrate the depths of this canyon—from its gates near Riverside Campground to its mouth at the Warm River confluence. Within this reach are unique natural features such as the 700 foot deep canyon, Sheep Falls, Upper and Lower Mesa Falls, and that small put potent capsizer of boats known as Surprise Falls. Within this canyon is a superb fishery because of the isolation. Rainbow trout ranging up to double figure poundage are in the pools and deep runs. Vast numbers of giant and golden stoneflies and baitfish make up the bulk of their diet, but many other species of stoneflies as well as those of caddisflies and mayflies are present. Large attractor patterns, wet or dry, are most effective in these swift and powerful waters, and during the emergence of the large stoneflies in June, attractors that imitate adults and nymphs take the largest trout of the season for those willing to spend the effort. Of course the most effective way to fish these waters is from a boat if one is aware of the location of the dangerous falls the rapids in the canyon. It is quite possible that more large trout reside in Cardiac Canyon, simply because of its isolation, than in any other reach of the river.

Upstream of Cardiac Canyon the river moderates in flow through the Riverside Campground-Pinehaven area. The variety of aquatic insects also changes in this transition area with larger stoneflies becoming less numerous and mayflies increasing in abundance as one travels upstream. Trout in good numbers, with some individuals attaining large sizes, reside here.

From Pinehaven to Island Park Dam is the combination of water types that has given the Henry's Fork fame as a fishery. This combination is almost unique, at least with respect to extent. The lower end of the reach, within Harriman State Park and the Harriman East property is the most renowned piece of meadow stream in the fly fishing world. Here the river winds through sagebrush and grasslands. It is mostly wadeable, but there are holes and runs of considerable depth in its nine mile course through the park and ad-

Kokanee, the land-locked version of sockeye salmon, provide an important part of the sport fishery in Island Park Reservoir. Individuals up to four pounds have been caught here. Smaller kokanee are forage for rainbow trout. Beginning in late August kokanee enter the river to ascend the Coffee Pot Canyon and pass through the Mack's Inn area. From here they move to spawning sites in the river below Big Springs, in the Henry's Lake Outlet, in Lucky Dog Creek and in Moose Creek. Many are intercepted by Idaho Department of Fish and Game personnel who trap them to obtain eggs and sperm for generating fish which are returned to the system, or used to replenish stocks at other sites or start kokanee populations elsewhere. Ken Retallic

Upper Mesa Falls is a well-known landmark in the Cardiac Canyon of the Henry's Fork. Its 114-foot drop makes it the highest waterfall in eastern Idaho, and just over a mile below the river drops 65 feet over Lower Mesa Falls. Bruce Staples

Late summer and early winter views of Sawtell Peak from the Henry's Fork below the Henry's Lake outlet confluence provide seasonal moods for the angler. The Tubs, haven for large rainbow, whitefish and occasional brook trout and cutthroat trout escapees from Henry's Lake, are the main angling features here. The rewards of fishing the Tubs were described decades ago by writers such as Ray Bergman and Alexander McDonald. More recently, Charlie Brooks describes them in his spell binding book The Henry's Fork. *Bruce Staples*

jacent lands. This low gradient water continues through the park past Osborne Bridge (U.S. Highway 20). Above the bridge is a brief fall of rapids, followed by a mile-long run through a pine forest. Then the river breaks out again into a large open meadow as it passes the buildings of the former Railroad Ranch owned until 1977 by the Harriman family. Continuing upstream the river maintains its low gradient characteristics (except for a brief rapids just above the buildings at the site of a service road bridge), through the upper end of the park and on through the reach past the sub-community of Island Park Village known as Last Chance.

Caddisflies and mayflies are so abundant that either species alone would provide a well stocked larder for the large number of trout residing in this reach. Quite possibly no other water in the world can match the abundance and variety of these two aquatic insect forms. For this beneficial occurance of stream, trout and insect life there was a unique individual who in the minds of many anglers will be forever linked with these waters.

The late Bing Lempke was the first angler not only to systematically study the mayfly population of this reach and to dispense his great store of knowledge of it, but also was the first uniquely creative fly tier to simulate the adult forms of these insects. Sensitive, inquisitive and animated he plied these waters for

decades, not only enjoying the matchless fly fishing but observing and analyzing the life cycles of mayflies and their effects on feeding habits of resident trout. He also discussed the behavior of resident mayflies with other anglers and contributed his knowledge to the fly fishing public. His presence on these waters was a tradition and fly fishers flocked to him to gain information on what was currently catching trout. With spirit and pleasure he conversed with beginner and expert alike dispensing information on such topics as which mayfly was emerging at the moment, how long it would continue to do so, and the fly patterns one should use to simulate the mayflies that trout were keying on. When challenged he defended his positions with tenacity and colorful language. The patterns he recommended for use were mainly his own creations, and they became known and used by large numbers of fly fishers in the area. Thus the effectiveness of Bing's patterns became part of the area's lore, and to many anglers his flies are expressions of art. My conversations with Bing usually occurred in his home or at fly fishing or fly tying events that we both attended.

"Bruce, the major mayfly emergences up there behave as systematically as anything in nature!" he exclaimed in his active manner. "Sure, they vary a bit in timing because of changes in weather or the amount of water present in the stream, but at any time during the season there is a characteristic suite of mayflies on the water at a given time of day. Then there are certain species that will emerge after it and those which have preceded it." Then almost characteristically he would add, "Look now, I've done nothing special that anyone else can't do if they are willing to put in some time to observe the emergences and do a little homework to identify each one!

The late Bing Lempke was not only a world renowned fly tier but a beloved and unique personality. His contributions to fly tying, fly fishing and aquatic entomology benefit all anglers. Bing was the nineteenth recipient of the Buz Buszek Memorial award for fly tying excellence. Dan Stoddard

Part of the lure of Henry's Lake is the large numbers of brook trout. The Idaho state record brook trout, seven pounds, nine ounces came from the Henry's Lake. Bruce Staples

"As far as the major mayfly species go, here is what you can expect to see from the season opener at the end of May on through October," he began. "Late in May the olive dun, as we call *Rithrogenia hageni*, emerges. At about the same time you will see pale morning duns *(Ephermerella infrequens, inermis, lacustrus)* emerge. Actually they continue to emerge through summer, and as time progresses the duns get smaller. As the middle of June passes the green drake *(Drunella grandis)* emergence peaks, and with it comes the crowds of fly fishers. This emergence is soon followed by the brown drake *(Ephemera simulans)*. On days in late June fish pale morning duns early in the day, green drakes in the middle and brown drakes in the evening. As green drakes decrease in numbers during the beginning of July slate wing olives *(Drunella flavilinea)* come on to give good late afternoon fishing. About mid July the slate cream duns *(Epeorus albertae)* and speckled duns *(Callibaetis* species) emerge followed by the mahogany duns *(Paraleptophlebia* species), which like the tricos *(Tricorythodes* species) and tiny blue winged olives *(Pseudocloeon edmundsi)*, begin to emerge and last into autumn. In autumn one of the largest resident mayflies, the gray drake *(Siphlonurus occidentalis)*, will be on the water. All season you will see various blue winged olives *(Baetis sp.)* on the water, and remember that with the shortening days and cooler nights you will see these late season emergences occurring closer to the middle of the day. If fishing mayfly emergers, duns and spinners is not for you, then fishing caddis patterns is another option. Many species of caddis emerge in large numbers all season long. Midges, stoneflies, damselflies and terrestrials are also present in good numbers."

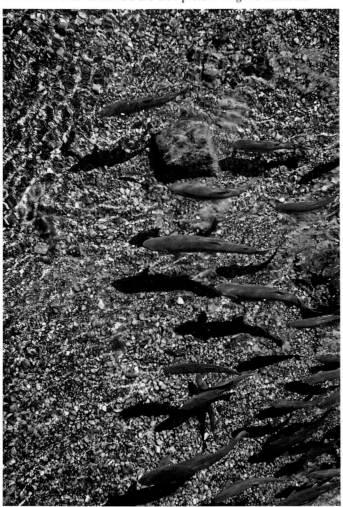

Upstream of the Last Chance-Harriman State Park waters is the famous three-mile long Box Canyon. It offers a fabulous population of caddisflies, mayflies and smaller stoneflies, but above all giant and golden stoneflies. In season, trout residing below the Island Park Dam come here to feed on the emerging giant and golden stoneflies. Then many move below to take advantage of vast mayfly and caddisfly emergences. Late in the season many trout move back to the canyon waters to feed on stonefly nymphs and bait fish. Many stay through winter, secure in the abundant and deep holding water. This habitat is of such a high quality that more than a few trout grow to enormous size. Individuals exceeding 15 pounds are known to inhabit the best locations. Few of these large trout are taken from these powerful waters, but one always has a chance to do so with large, deeply fished streamers and nymphs, particularly in late autumn, however, other seasons provide easier action.

The Buffalo River, which enters Henry's Fork a few hundred yards below Island Park Dam, holds large numbers of small brook and rainbow trout eager to take small dry flies. Perhaps the best time to fish the Box Canyon waters with large dry flies is during the June giant and golden stonefly emergence. Large nymph patterns work well in riffles and runs not only at this time, but throughout summer and autumn, particularly on overcast days. During these times terrestrial patterns including ants, beetles, crickets, wasps and hoppers take fish from the canyon waters as well as from the Last Chance-Harriman State Park waters downstream.

The bountiful water from Harriman State Park to Box Canyon has also produced an abundance of exceptional fly fishers. One must go to legendary Michigan or Pennsylvania streams, New York's Catskills, or western Montana rivers to find anglers with equal skill. Bing Lempke's name will always be synonymous with these waters. So will that of Rene Harrop, the gifted artist, fly fisher, and fly tier from St. Anthony. Rene and his wife Bonnie are renown for their beautiful artwork and for creating fly patterns that are not only effective in these waters but in trout streams worldwide. Much of their inspiration must have come from the quality of the Island Park waters; for it is here that they have fished and observed various hatches for years. Mike Lawson is also synonymous with these waters. Mike, a native of Sugar City, and his wife, Sheralee, own The Henry's Fork Anglers (a quality fly fishing shop at Last Chance). Mike has also spent decades accumulating knowledge about fishing these water and shares it willingly and pleasantly with others. In a sense these waters, perhaps the best example of large stream quality in the world, have had a synergistic effect by producing outstanding contributors to the art of fly fishing. These anglers are also in the forefront of those protecting the water's quality. One must consider that if there had been no quality to these waters, what would have happened to the contributions from the Harrops, Lawsons, and Lempkes?

Above Box Canyon, a portion of the Henry's Fork is inundated by Island Park Reservoir which began impounding water in May of 1939, and has had a negative effect on downstream habitat because it is used to fluctuate water flows to meet irrigation demands, thus interrupting spawning runs. Along with the

The waters of Big Springs provide most of the volume for the upper Henry's Fork. The high quality waters down to the Henry's Lake Outlet confluence provide a trout sanctuary. Fishing is not allowed here, so at the Big Springs Bridge one finds east Idaho's best natural trout viewing site. These residents function as brood stock for the upper river and serve as a reminder of what trout populations could be when conditions are unspoiled. Bruce Staples

negative effects created by the dam is the certainty of other problems if a proposed new hydropower plant is added. The reservoir behind the dam has never provided an outstanding fishery because of drawdowns and the introduction of rough fish. Sadly, the now submerged Henry's Fork, its feeder streams and private impoundments historically offered a higher quality fishery than the large reservoir.

A fine Harriman Park rainbow being pictured before release. Originally the Henry's Fork was inhabited by cutthroat trout. Rainbows were introduced throughout the river early in this century, and over the years have hybridized with original cutthroat stocks. Thus most rainbows in the river are hybrids, and they range upward to sizes that make the Henry's Fork a world renowned cold water fishery. Mike Lawson

Shotgun Creek, now submerged in the broad west arm of the reservoir, collected tributaries from the Centennial Range and Thurmon Ridge, then entered Henry's Fork from the west. It was an outstanding fishery in the past, and a few anglers still recall the huge rainbow and cutthroat trout that resided in the bends and impoundments of this sinuous tributary to the Henry's Fork. Mill Creek on the east, to Sheridan Creek on the west, provide good fishing for small brook trout and large rainbow that occasionally escape from private impoundments. Good sport can be found in Island Park Reservoir, particularly on the west end in the Grizzly Springs area, and along the south shoreline bays locally known as "The Fingers." Leech, streamer and nymph patterns fished from a float tube work well.

Above Island Park Reservoir the river flows through Coffee Pot Canyon, a three mile gorge crowned near its top with the steep and scenic Coffee Pot Rapids. As with the Box Canyon below the reservoir, vast numbers of large stoneflies are present. During their early and mid June emergence fishing with large dry flies or nymphs becomes an exhilarating experience. At other times fishing the abundant pocket water with dry attractor patterns can be effective. But nymph and streamer fishing produces best throughout the season. Fishing these waters with wet flies for late season run-up rainbows from the reservoir can be particularly rewarding. Many of the rainbows follow kokanee spawning runs to the Big Springs area and the Moose Creek drainage or are participating in their own spawning run. In size and strength they rival trout in the Box Canyon below. These run-ups have been fished over for decades, and tales of fishing for them go back to the early twentieth century and

are mentioned in Alexander MacDonald's *On Becoming A Fly Fisherman.*

Above the Coffee Pot area the river slows to flows similar to those in the Last Chance-Harriman State Park reach but there is less natural cover. The fishery is somewhat degraded by heavy stocking of hatchery reared catchables and by the passage of power boats. Private clubs, including the Flat Rock Club, are located on these waters. About three miles above this site the river runs through a unique area of bogs and meadows that harbor several large, deep holes known as "The Tubs." The first of The Tubs is located at the confluence of the Henry's Fork with the west fork of the Henry's Lake Outlet, and the one farthest upstream is located at the river's confluence with the east fork of the outlet. In these holes large rainbow, brook, cutthroat and whitefish reside year-round, but in late autumn the run of rainbows from Island Park Reservoir adds good numbers of exceptional fish. Above this reach is the Big Springs sanctuary, which is an intrusion free spawning and rearing area as well as an area in which to observe the behavior of trout in a beautiful natural setting. Most of the river's volume comes from these springs. The springs' water is nearly free of nutrients because it originates in rhyolitic country rock. Thus,

Float tubers and boaters on Henry's Lake may enjoy such calm periods but must remain wary of winds that can whistle without warning from Red Rock Pass to the southwest or Raynolds Pass to the northwest and alter this idyllic setting. Dennis Bitton

Sawtell Peak, a major landmark in the Centennial Range on the Idaho-Montana border, holds a cap of snow that reminds spring-time Henry's Fork anglers at Last Chance that winter is only a few thousand feet above. Early season emergence of the olive dun, pale morning dun and caddis species bring good numbers of anglers to the Henry's Fork at Last Chance. Just below is the Harriman State Park reach holding a phenomenal green drake population. Tantalizingly closed until mid June, the park waters are accessed via Last Chance by most anglers. Dennis Bitton

Henry's Fork becomes a rich stream farther downsteam as it flows over rock that gives up nutrients more readily.

Some assert that Henry's Lake Outlet is a tributary to the main river which, they say, emerges from Big Springs. Officially the outlet is the Henry's Fork, although its physical form is smaller and quite different than any downstream reach. Between Henry's Lake and the Big Springs Outlet much of the Henry's Fork is a riffle and run meadow stream with pools as it courses Henry's Lake Flat. Here it has been degraded somewhat by heavy livestock usage and flow fluctuations from Henry's Lake Dam, which was constructed to store irrigation water. Nevertheless, wet and terrestrial patterns are productive in the outlet, through the meadow, and below in the bogs thick with willows. Residents are mainly cutthroat and brook trout and some attain large sizes. Both walk in and float fishing are effective in the outlet, but the bogs and thick willows hinder both methods at the lower end of the reach.

Atop the Henry's Fork, situated in a bowl rimmed on three sides by mountains forming the Continental Divide, is Henry's Lake. Fed by springs and headwater streams Henry's Lake is a veritable fish factory with a bounty of brook, cutthroat, hybrid, rainbow trout and more recently an unwanted token of brown trout. As with the entire Henry's Fork the original inhabitants were cutthroat trout, but escapee rainbow and brook trout from private hatcheries and other introductions have also populated the lake. Now few lakes of similar size can boast the renown of Henry's Lake, with its cutthroat and hybrid trout ranging into double figure poundage and brook trout approaching eight pounds.

Henry's Lake also provides an excellent example of a fishery enhanced by a dam. Before a dam for storing irrigation water was built on its outlet in 1923 the lake had an average depth of five feet. It held a good fishery, though it was limited by a wide seasonal water temperature fluctuations causing winter kills and summer oxygen deficiencies. The dam's impounded water increased the average depth to 12 feet, not only moderating the water temperature but greatly increasing the lake's surface area which is primarily over shallow areas and produces an abundance of aquatic insects.

As with all lakes the best fly fishing strategy is to cast wet flies from a boat or float tube. Many patterns are effective on Henry's Lake, but generally one will find that leech and scud patterns produce year-round. During late June to mid July the damsel fly emergence makes fishing nymph imitations important in the shallower areas and over springs. Then, as late season approaches, streamers become more effective—particularly when brook trout spawning runs begin along the north shore. At this time a boat or float tube is not required. In late October wet flies cast while wading the north shore can be as productive as any other method.

Happily, Henry's Lake appears to have a bright future because its value to the eastern Idaho economy is being recognized. There are advocacy groups now monitoring it. Solutions are being sought for the introduction of nutrients that cause algae blooms. Fisheries management practices and a considerate attitude from the irrigation company that controls its water volume have combined to provide even more protection. Private land owners are adopting grazing and water use practices that give tributary streams a quality that allows significant spawning. In addition to being a premier fishery Henry's Lake is becoming a success story of cooperation by different interest groups working together to protect a quality natural resource.

THE SOUTH FORK OF THE SNAKE RIVER

At the base of Menan Buttes, the right hand, or easterly branch of the Snake River is known as the South Fork to most east Idahoans. It flows from a high country source near Yellowstone National Park and through Wyoming. Being the major branch it is therefore the Snake River proper. On its course through Wyoming and into Idaho it receives high country drainages from the Teton, Gros Ventre, Wyoming, Salt, Snake River, Caribou and Big Hole ranges making it a runoff stream of large proportions. This condition gives it a different suite of aquatic insects, particularly mayfly species, than found in the Henry's Fork. For example, species living in silty or sandy bottoms are relatively scarce because the habitat they require is largely removed by its swift waters. And because of the uncertainties of runoff, emergences of aquatic insects common to both streams occur later and with more variability than in the Henry's Fork. One good example is in the emergence of large stonefly species, *Pteronarcys californica* and *Acroneuria californica*, the giant and golden stones. Emergence of these two species occurs from late May through late June on the Henry's Fork, but on the

colder runoff laden South Fork emergence usually occurs from late June through July.

The South Fork is also greatly affected by the management of two upstream irrigation storage reservoirs: Jackson Lake in Jackson Hole, Wyoming and Palisades Reservoir which submerges its course for nearly 20 miles, as well as that of the lower Salt River, after entering Idaho. Palisades Reservoir offers little consistent sport to the fly fisher not equipped with streamer flies and a boat or float tube. Brown trout that run up the Salt River from Palisades Reservoir in mid and late September offer anglers some sport on the upper end. The reservoir decreases siltation in the river below, but in general it has no other beneficial effects—particularly when water releases are erratically and abruptly managed almost to Labor Day in most years. Throughout its nearly 70 mile reach from Palisades Dam to its confluence with the Henry's Fork the South Fork is similar with respect to appearance, however the countryside changes. Whether it flows through Swan Valley, Conant Valley, its canyon or out onto the Snake River Plain it is a repetition of

Brown trout, like this one being returned, are becoming increasingly common in the South Fork of the Snake River. In lower reaches of the river they outnumber native cutthroat trout. Jimmy Gabettas

In early September cottonwoods begin to change summer greens for autumn golds along the South Fork Canyon. Land purchases by the Nature Conservancy and sympathetic individuals help preserve the canyon for all forms of wildlife. Bruce Staples

pools, riffles and runs interspersed with productive channel areas. A little known fact is that with respect to dissolved nutrients it is richer than the Henry's Fork. But this favorable condition for quality cold water fisheries is offset by its runoff load and the almost wild variability in its flows. Throughout the river trout can be taken if one presents imitations of seasonally available aquatic insects, streamers or terrestrial life forms and avoids fishing during and right after abrupt changes in flow.

For the purpose of this book the South Fork can be divided into two general reaches based on degradation by man. Going upstream the first is from the confluence with the Henry's Fork and ends at the last in the series of major irrigation diversions a few miles above the Heise Hot Springs Resort where the South Fork leaves its magnificent canyon. This reach features large scale degradation caused by irrigation diversions which can take water any time in low water years and late into years of normal water flows. Dewatering, siltation from agricultural practices and heavy fishing pressure from nearby towns have combined to reduce the native strains of cutthroat in the reach to a remnant of historic levels. A large population of whitefish remains, and over the years other strains of cutthroat, brown and some rainbow trout have been introduced into the river to absorb the effects of degradation. What remains of this potentially highly productive fishery is a remnant, but it is still worthy of one's attention because of its good population of now dominant brown trout, ranging up to trophy size, and cutthroat trout.

The South Fork reach running from the mouth of the canyon upstream to Palisades Dam is less impacted by man and a better population of native cutthroat trout survives. Rainbows are found in the upper end of the reach, trophy size browns throughout and whitefish in abundance. Roads parallel most of the river making walk-in access fairly easy. But it is from boat, canoe or raft that one can best fish this big water, especially during the stonefly season. In fact it is the only practical way to fish the essentially roadless area from Conant Valley down to the end of the South Fork Road at Black Canyon. In this beautiful and almost pristine area one experiences a remnant of the river's state in the early nineteenth century when those plying the fur trade from the east used the river as a corridor to reach the Snake River Plain and the beaver rich highlands to the east and south. In those days the only salmonids present in the river were whitefish and fine and large spotted strains of cutthroat trout. The trout were named "salmon trout" by the trappers and explorers and undoubtedly provided them with many a meal.

Degradation of the river began in the 1870s when huge livestock herds were trailed alongside it to the ranges in Wyoming. Pioneer activities such as logging and farming in the Poplar area above Heise and in Conant and Swan valleys added to the degradation, mainly through siltation. Canals to provide water for agricultural purposes tapped the lower river and the long history of negative effects on the fishery started. Nevertheless, a fine fishery existed in the river for nearly a century. It was after the completion of Palisades Dam in 1956 when the serious decline of the native cutthroat population in the entire river began. Cutthroat numbers were affected by variable flows and the change in water properties caused by the dam. The canyon, for example, was the population center for a strain of cutthroat that regularly produced immense individuals. Members of this strain migrated upriver into Wyoming during spawning season until Palisades Dam barred passage in

1956. It is uncertain whether this strain still exists but if so it is reduced to a token, because today cutthroats over 10 pounds are rare throughout the South Fork. Currently, the canyon section, and, in fact, the whole reach in Idaho is in peril because of nearly ideal dam sites in the canyon above Heise.

For decades downstream water users have coveted dams to provide dry year reserves or waters for future agricultural development. It matters little that further agricultural development is senseless considering the present overabundance of products, or that because of prior water rights it would take years to fill reservoirs that would inundate the entire reach well into Swan Valley. Yet in the face of bald impracticality, the loss of a great source of growing recreation dollars and of increasingly rare good quality water, the clamor to dam goes on—ebbing in years of abundant snowfall and increasing to the gates of frenzy in years of drought. Without dam building, management practices of Palisades Reservoir and Jackson Lake and further development on private lands from the canyon to Swan Valley will cloud the river's future. There is much to lose. This is eastern Idaho's largest and potentially most productive trout stream. There are those who believe that with proper management of flows this river could support a fishery excelling Henry's Fork in the Island Park area. After all, it consistently produces the Idaho record brown trout with the latest individual weighing just below 35 pounds!

Facing page:

A summer evening caddis emergence on the South Fork has rewards that go beyond fishing. Jimmy Gabettas

Majestic and endangered, the bald eagle inhabits pristine reaches of the Henry's Fork, the South Fork of the Snake River, the Teton River, Falls River and others. The bald eagle's presence is a true measure of total quality in any fishery, so no contemplative angler begrudges this endangered native his share of fish. Considerate recreationists alter their behavior to protect the eagle and increasingly support efforts to preserve its vital habitat throughout eastern Idaho. Michael B. Whitfield

Fall colors make a float trip on the South Fork of the Snake River a memorable event regardless of cooperation of trout and whitefish. Increasingly sightseers float the river to enjoy scenery such as Mount Baldy presiding over September's golden cottonwoods in Swan Valley. Dennis Bitton

For decades the quality fishery of the South Fork of the Snake River was essentially an eastern Idaho secret. Visiting anglers flocked to the Henry's Fork or Henry's Lake, both deservedly heralded as fishing utopias. The secret of the South Fork was revealed only recently. Now, from the late June giant stonefly emergence through October it receives more angler attention than any body of water in eastern Idaho. The scene here is in Swan Valley and is typical of the river and surroundings in July. Floating anglers, regardless of terminal gear, sample the effects of the giant and golden stonefly emergence on brown, cutthroat and rainbow trout. The cutthroat, represented by the elegant Snake River fine spotted sub-species, is native. Browns were introduced earlier in the century and now grow to sizes exceeding thirty pounds! Rainbows, more recently introduced, grow to several pounds and are becoming common in the Swan Valley area. The South Fork is big water. It is also capable of being the best trout stream in the Rocky Mountains, if managed to favor the fishery. However, private homesites have damaged its riparian zones of willows and cottonwoods. Irrigation demands have distorted its natural water volumes and Palisades Dam blocks migration of its trout population. Thus man has degraded its natural state and also will decide its future quality. Frank Amato

Thus the South Fork holds brown trout to world class size, cut-throat trout to double figure poundage, east Idaho's largest trout population, a rich variety of caddisflies, mayflies and stoneflies, a giant and golden stonefly emergence of huge proportion, a variety of water types and unparalleled scenery. Why then has it not received as much acclaim as Henry's Fork in the Island Park area? The best reason is geographic and quite common in the development of the western United States. A railroad was built across the Island Park area in 1907 to bring visitors to the west entrance of Yellowstone National Park. Using this railroad was an affluent and literate influx of sportsmen who not only visited retreats such as on the Trude and Harriman properties in Island Park, but publicized the area's fisheries and established fishing camps and private clubs on the banks of Henry's Fork. The result for Henry's Fork in this area was a glittering and well deserved reputation as a fishery long before massive use of the automobile.

A railroad built by the Harriman family also developed the Sun Valley area and Silver Creek's reputation as a fishery in Central Idaho. No railroad was built into the upper valleys of the South Fork of the Snake River. Thus, there was no early influx of outside sportsmen to build a reputation for the South Fork. When sportsmen came in large numbers to fish the South Fork, it was not only well after the establishment of modern highways in the 1940s, but long after the Henry's Fork had established its reputation. Now the South Fork's fishery is being heralded in outdoor magazines, videos and television. To serve the resultant and increasing influx of anglers several fishing guides and tackle shops have established businesses along its course. Visitors now come by air and auto from all over the world to enjoy its waters—mainly by boat fishing. This influx has another benefit for the South Fork. Advocate groups to protect its fishery are becoming robust. These groups now challenge abrupt management of flows out of Palisades Reservoir and Jackson Lake. By purchasing riverfront and adjacent lands along the canyon they are protecting the priceless fishery and wildlife habitat. They also demand management practices that will protect the fishery in the light of increased pressure from anglers, developers and irrigators alike. Much of the South Fork's future is in the hands of these groups. Let us hope that their efforts will at least maintain the present water quality, and let us accept the fact that publicity about the South Fork's fishery will be the mechanism that protects its quality.

HIGHLAND DRAINAGES

A brief look at a relief map of eastern Idaho shows mountain ranges forming a semicircle around the eastern expanse of the Snake River Plain. These geographic features force drainages originating in the mountain ranges and higher valleys to flow westerly into canyons to feed the trunk streams on the plain below. The effect created is similar to that of a series of troughs feeding one side of a basin that is drained by one larger outlet on the other side. More than 10,000 square miles of convoluted land with mountains up to 10,000 feet high make up the eastern Idaho highlands. This is classic western high country in every sense—mountains with higher slopes holding stands of pines bordered at lower elevation by magnificent quaking aspen groves and brushy bench lands. The streams range in size up to moderate rivers and are contained in all types of settings—defiles, canyons, verdant willow enriched meadows and stark sagebrush flats. Away from the mountain slopes most stretches are of moderate gradient to little at all. In general riparian zones and irregular surface features provide good instream cover which is supplemented generously by beaver ponds in settings having ample willow and quaking aspen and an easy stream gradient.

It was the dense population of beavers that brought the first fingers of western civilization to exploit this land in the early nineteenth century. Vast numbers of beavers were trapped to be made into mode of the day headgear. Beavers still survive in good numbers and benefit the fisheries because their ponds offer cover and habitat, and they also help regulate water flow. But it is the underlying geology that provides the basis for the rich natural state of the highland streams.

Osprey are coming back in good numbers to isolated waterways in eastern Idaho. Like the bald eagle they also benefit from the growing habitat preservation movement and conservation awareness in the area. Orlyn Gaddis

Elk are common in the mountains and highlands throughout eastern Idaho. On autumn evenings the sounds of bugling bulls mixes with honking of migrating geese and the coyote's howl to give the outdoorsman the best of natures' serenades. Ken Retallic

Nearly the entire area is underlaid by fractured, permeable lava and sedimentary rock rich in carbonates and phosphates usable for building food chains. Abundant snowfall from long winters results in a downward percolation of melt waters throughout the country. These waters dissolve nutrients and reappear as numerous springs to recharge the highland streams with the richest waters anywhere. All bases for a marvelous fishery are found here. Major aquatic life forms are abundantly available for trout. Freestone riffles and runs provide vast quantities of stoneflies, mayflies, midges, caddisflies and snails. Lower gradient waters and ponds provide generous amounts of mayflies, midges, dragonflies, damselflies, craneflies, leeches and scuds. Terrestrial and vertebrate life forms are found throughout. Thus native cutthroat trout prospered, and in the unaltered fisheries of the past were frequently present in great numbers with some individuals attaining large sizes.

Only a fraction of the amount of water is diverted from the highland streams for irrigation in comparison to that diverted from the trunk streams below. But riparian zone destruction by grazing and timbering have degraded certain sections of streambeds, and in the more westerly and southerly portion of the highlands siltation from poor agricultural practices has despoiled many reaches. It is still the occasional low snowfall winters, however, that have the most serious negative effects on highland fisheries. Nevertheless highland fisheries are still eminently worthy of exploration. In recent decades brook, brown and rainbow trout have been introduced to supplement the native cutthroat in certain streams and reservoirs. These imports sometimes grow to trophy sizes. The presence of trout in a variety of remote waters in beautiful settings will bring one back to the highlands for quality times. You may find your special place here so let's have a closer look.

WARM RIVER DRAINAGE

Warm River originates from springs near the western base of the Madison Plateau, then flows south to its confluence with the Henry's Fork. Other than timbering activities in areas away from water courses, little significant alteration has been made to Warm River and its tributaries. Merely a creek in its upper reaches, Warm River and its main tributary, Partridge Creek, offer brook trout in abundance. Both streams, however, receive little attention because of their proximity to the Henry's Fork.

After flowing about three miles this small river is enhanced by Warm River Spring, which more than doubles its flow. Abandoned Warm River Hatchery at the spring is one of the most picturesque settings one will find and is an enjoyable destination for an easy afternoon outing. For about three miles downstream from this spot is good riffle, run and pocket water, best fished with attractor and dry caddis patterns for small, eager rainbow and brook trout. Access to this section is gained from a good gravel road that turns east off the Mesa Falls Scenic Loop just above the upper falls and ends at the hatchery. One can also access Warm River above its cascades

by driving south of the hatchery access road and travelling with care down the old railroad grade for about a mile to a gate, then wading into the canyon. Below the cascades Warm River is in a steep canyon that is best approached by walking up the railroad grade from the forest service campground. Here the river is in a lovely setting, and there is good fishing for juvenile brown trout (spawned from Henry's Fork residents), native and stocked rainbows, and an occasional brook trout—small dry flies work best. But it is usually crowded with weekenders until after Labor Day making September the best time to fish. After September the lower river is closed to fishing to protect spawning Henry's Fork browns. Three Rivers Ranch is just below the campground on the point of land between the Warm River/Robinson Creek confluence, not far from where Warm River empties into Henry's Fork.

The best access to Robinson Creek is found if one makes a right onto Fish Creek Road at the entrance to Warm River Campground, travels four miles, then turns right on a graveled forest service road to Robinson Creek Canyon. From here the creek can be

Warm River in winter. Below Warm River Spring, site of an old state fish hatchery, the river is paralleled by the railroad line to West Yellowstone. Now abandoned, the railroad bed is travelled by cross country skiers and snowmobilers who enjoy some unique winter scenery. Bruce Staples

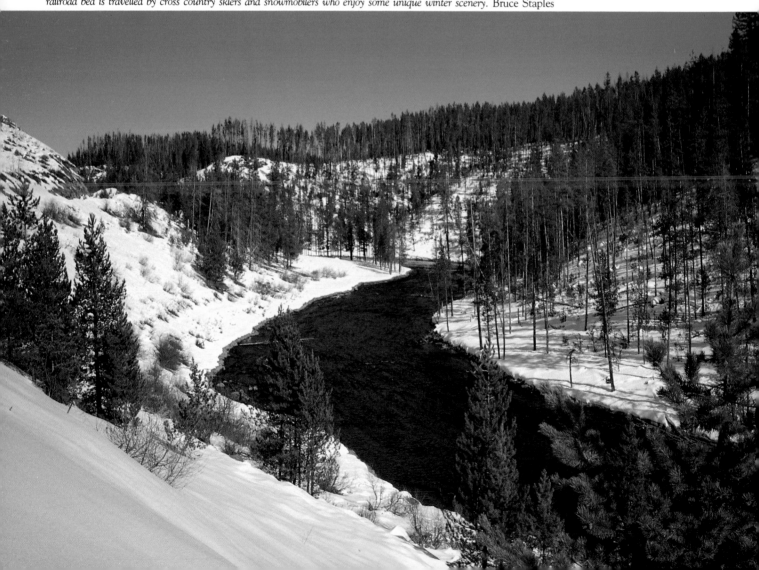

Back to live another day! This rainbow is returned to its habitat. With increasing size and age it will seek bigger water and thus move downstream to the Henry's Fork.
Jimmy Gabettas

fished at several points. The road goes on to cross the creek and then intersects the Green Timber Road leading to Cave Falls on Falls River. In this area Robinson Creek is a delight, especially when fished in late afternoons during June and July. One never knows if cutthroat, brook, brown, cutthroat-rainbow hybrid or rainbow trout will rise to strike a fly, and one must be alert because there are a few residents that exceed two pounds.

Robinson Creek originates on the southwest edge of Madison Plateau in Yellowstone National Park, and therefore carries a runoff load that in normal snowfall years ebbs by mid June. At this time of warming water an emergence of aquatic insects equivalent to those found in the Henry's Fork in variety, but unrivaled in numbers by any stream of similar size occurs. Excellent numbers of giant, golden and smaller stoneflies are found along with mayflies from pale morning duns and blue winged olives to green drakes.

Huge numbers of caddisflies also emerge. The amount of these insects dwindle by the end of July but by then terrestrial insects have built good populations. Farther upstream, Robinson Creek is contained in a nearly inaccessible canyon which can be entered from the Cave Falls Road at two points: by a road going north just past the Rock Creek crossing, and by a steep foot path at the end of Horseshoe Lake Road. At this point one finds lesser numbers of browns and rainbows but even greater numbers of cutthroat and brook trout eager for any fly offered. If one seeks smaller streams, Rock, Porcupine and Wyoming creeks, all just off Cave Falls Road, offer large populations of pan-sized brook trout and solitude in an unspoiled setting. In recent years Horseshoe Lake has hosted a novelty: grayling planted by the Idaho Department of Fish and Game.

FALLS RIVER DRAINAGE

Until recently Falls River has had a status problem simply because of its proximity to a fabulously productive reach of Henry's Fork. But with the gradual loss of quality trout waters more attention is being given by anglers and fisheries managers to overlooked waters. This is the case with Falls River, and the quality of its fishery has not been realized. Within its 35 mile reach in Idaho it is almost entirely a rainbow trout fishery. Its trout population does not equal Henry's Fork; nevertheless it contains individuals whose size rivals those of the largest rainbows found in the nearby legendary river.

Falls River is mainly confined to a box canyon as it flows from heavily timbered ridges to cut a southwesterly groove across the grain and potato fields of southern Fremont County. It breaks out of its canyon about three miles east of the community of Chester, and from there flows across the Snake River Plain for a few miles to meet Henry's Fork just above Chester Diversion Dam. Throughout its entire length it is a moderately sized freestone stream with a succession of riffles, runs, pools and pocket water punctuated with steep rapids. In its upper reach, close to the Wyoming border, its gradient

is steeper; some of its rapids border on being cascades. At least two water falls, Sheep Falls and another unnamed at Dog Creek, prevent upstream migration of whitefish and trout.

Throughout most of its course in Idaho one finds a good population of giant and golden stoneflies and volumes of caddisflies. However high its water quality or rich its aquatic insect life there are basic reasons why it cannot be as productive as the adjacent reaches of the Henry's Fork. Its headwaters drain the Madison and Pitchstone plateaus in Yellowstone National Park and the northwest slope of the Teton Range. Thus Falls River is a major runoff stream. In most years runoff subsides from its reach in Idaho near the end of June or the beginning of July. This makes its warm water season four to six weeks less than that of the adjacent Henry's Fork above Chester. In addition, its principle upstream tributaries (Boundary Creek, Bechler River and Mountain Ash Creek) and its own origins drain country underlaid by relatively insoluble rhyolitic lavas which give up little in dissolved nutrients. Thus, its waters are lean until flows from richer ground and surface waters supplement its lower reaches. Nevertheless, its best popula-

Cave Falls, inside the Yellowstone National Parks southwest corner and just east of the Idaho-Wyoming border marks the gateway to Falls River Basin. Below, Falls River courses through Fremont county and holds not only a valuable rainbow fishery but economically vital irrigation water. Bruce Staples

Winter snows wrap Falls River just above the Kelly Bridge in eastern Fremont County. In the distance to the east is the north end of the Teton Range in Jedediah Smith Wilderness area. Bruce Staples

tions of rainbow and occasional cutthroat are found in the upper reaches in Idaho which are remote enough to remain in a natural state. Where the river could produce a denser population in its lower reaches, quality conditions are compromised by major irrigation diversions that progressively dewater its course down to the Henry's Fork, and by runoff from agricultural practices above the canyon walls. Now a six mile reach in the middle of the rivers course is threatened with dewatering to supply a hydropower project. Dewatering and agricultural runoff also affect its only major downstream tributary in Idaho, Conant Creek, which (along with Squirrel Creek and Boone Creek) holds good populations of brook trout and cutthroat trout in its upper reaches.

But do not let this discourse discourage you, because Falls public land for access throughout its reach in Idaho, and when asked, private land owners usually grant permission to access the river. Fish its entire length with adult and nymph stonefly and caddisfly imitations during and after their emergence in June and July. Then, as summer develops, switch to terrestrial patterns and streamers through the fall season. You will surely obtain the same degree of success found on the adjacent reach of Henry's Fork.

River has significant advantages when compared to the adjacent Henry's Fork. You are sure to find solitude at most locations along its course, as well as a good population of rainbow that are not fished over with the intensity found on Henry's Fork. There is much

Falls River Canyon offers superb scenery and rainbow trout to several pounds. Late summer to early autumn is the best time to fish this powerful water in a wilderness setting. Bruce Staples

TETON RIVER DRAINAGE

The Teton River burst into national prominence on Saturday, June 5, 1976 with the tragic failure of Teton Dam. This recent catastrophe has greatly altered much of the river in the canyon and below.

In a physical sense Teton River is a model for the major east Idaho highland streams. Its sources, high country streams and springs, flow into an upland valley to form the stream. From here it flows into a canyon and then descends onto the plain below. As with Falls River the Teton carries spring runoff throughout its course making its warm water season shorter than that of the Henry's Fork.

In the Snake River Plain, not far from where it exits its canyon, the Teton divides into north and south forks which enter the Henry's Fork after flowing entirely through land developed for agricultural and municipal purposes. Here the Teton is mending from the effects of the dam break but because of dewatering, pollution, riparian zone destruction and siltation it has a bleak future as a fishery compared to its upstream reaches.

Above the Snake River Plain the Teton flows for over 30 miles through an abrupt and isolated canyon. Until the construction of Teton Dam in the early 1970s, Teton Canyon was as uni-

que and beautiful as any canyon found in the West. It provided winter range for deer and elk, hosted a large variety of smaller wildlife and had a rich variety of flora. But the river was its gem. Below Felt Power Dam it flowed free through the deep canyon, except for a minor private impoundment that supplied irrigation water which was pumped up the canyon to the Linderman Ranch. To many the lower canyon was a smaller version of the one through which the South Fork of the Snake River flows on the other side of the Big Hole Range. Here was found the same nutrient rich, freestone stream with riffles, runs, pools and channels. The steeper upper canyon was, and remains, a wild water of boulders and rapids that challenges rafter and kayaker as well as the fly fisher. Throughout, the river hosted a healthy population of cutthroat and rainbow trout to trophy size and a few brook trout. Caddis and stonefly emergences from the canyon waters were legendary. In late spring when the water lowered and cleared immense numbers of giant and golden stoneflies were available to trout. This event was a happening for many local fisherman and a few knowledgeable outsiders. With word of stonefly sightings walk-in anglers and those with boats and rafts descended on the lower canyon, mainly through the Linderman Ranch, to float 17 miles to its mouth while experiencing superb fishing. The stonefly

Damage to the canyon can be seen from this aerial shot. When the Teton Dam failed on Saturday, June 5, 1976 the reservoir was about two-thirds filled. When it drained, canyon walls slumped into the river changing its nature forever. The fishery here is recovering but the canyon's beauty remains scarred. Bruce Staples

Bitch Creek, a lovely foothill stream and tributary to the Teton River, flows almost due west to meet the Teton River. In its upper reaches it holds only cutthroat trout, but as it slips into an ever-deepening canyon rainbows and cutthroat-rainbow hybrids occupy its choicest places. Bruce Staples

emergence ascended the canyon through waters difficult to float then spent itself above Felt Dam. Then, throughout summer and into autumn, caddisflies and terrestrial insects emerged throughout the canyon to provide excellent sport. The canyon up to the Bitch Creek confluence was changed dramatically by the dam's construction and failure. First, trees in the canyon below the high water line of the reservoir were cut down. By the beginning of June in 1976 water had been impounded to 60 percent capacity. Then, with the dam failure and subsequent rapid drop in water levels, the sodden, denuded slopes slumped into the canyon at several points causing landslides which dammed the river. The effect of this was to convert much of the river into a series of pools or long runs of slow moving water punctuated by cascades of water rushing over barriers formed by the landslides. This drowned many of the insect producing riffles and destroyed spawning habitat and holding water. A salmonid fishery remains and is improving, however, in the gutted canyon the Teton River will continue for decades to be only a remnant of what it once was.

In the canyon above this damaged area, and in Bitch Creek, much of the original fishery and aquatic insects remain. The fishery is comprised of nearly half whitefish with the rest being cutthroat, rainbow and a few brook trout. Much attention by fly fishers now, however, is given to the river in Teton Valley where it is more accessible. Here it is a classic meadow stream in a picturesque setting. It winds through mostly private lands, and permission to access the river is usually granted. In its course the river is joined by numerous springs and headwater streams from the Teton Range to the east and the Big Hole Range to the south and west. The river is generally shallow and of low gradient and, as with many of the headwater streams, holds a good number of small cutthroat and brook trout with an occasional rainbow. But it suffers from siltation accumulated by decades of poor grazing practices. This limits the amount of deep water cover available for large trout and has smothered spawning areas and productive aquatic insect habitat. Dewatering for irrigation also limits successful spawning in tributaries throughout the basin. Thus the productivity of this nutrient rich river is compromised. Nevertheless, fishing it for smaller trout and trophies in a uniquely beautiful setting attracts many walk-in and float fishers.

Cutthroat abound in the Teton River, but these colorful natives are common throughout eastern Idaho. Dennis Bitton

Jackson is to the east beyond the Teton Peaks. Looking up Teton Canyon from Idaho's Teton Basin one sees Mount Owen on the left, the Grand Teton in the middle and Middle Teton on the right. The Teton Range is a formidable barrier to storms coming from the west. Thus the Teton Range captures snows which melt to feed the Teton River drainage on the west as well as part of the Falls River drainage to the north. On the Jackson Hole side waters run from the Range to feed the Snake River locally called the South Fork when it enters Idaho. Dennis Bitton

SOUTH FORK TRIBUTARIES

Several streams with good populations of cutthroat feed nutrient rich waters into the South Fork of the Snake River during its northwesterly course past the Snake River, Caribou and Big Hole ranges in Bonneville County. All are freestone streams with moderate gradients and have good natural cover, rich aquatic insect life and are impared by agricultural or livestock usages. These tributaries can be divided into two groups: those contributing to the river below Palisades Dam, and those flowing into the reservoir above the dam.

Below the dam five streams (Palisades, Rainey, Pine, Pritchard and Burns creeks) provide spawning and rearing areas for river fish in addition to hosting their own populations. Much of Pine Creek is adjacent to State Highway 31 and therefore is heavily fished. In its extreme upper and lower portions, which are away from the highway, it holds some larger trout. Rainey Creek is easily fished in much of its canyon east of the town of Swan Valley. Here it holds small cutthroat. In the valley it flows through much private land but holds brown, cutthroat and some rainbow trout which can grow to very large size. Fall Creek holds small cutthroat trout but is blocked to usage by river fish because of a picturesque 30-foot waterfall at its mouth. Palisades Creek, five miles below the dam, is particularly important and unique. It is the largest downstream tributary, but its once considerable run of spawning cutthroat and the fry produced have been reduced by a major irrigation diversion not far from its mouth. The cost of effectively screening this diversion is high, but the benefit would be enormous in terms of adults

and fry returned to the river. Above this diversion the water in Palisades Creek is naturally regulated by Lower and Upper Palisades lakes, both formed by landslides eons ago. These picturesque lakes make the area a popular destination. The lower lake is a pleasant four mile hike over a well marked and maintained forest service trail along the creek. The lake itself can be fished from its inlet and from open areas along its southern shoreline. Nymph and leach patterns attract cutthroat that can attain surprising sizes. Above the lower lake one hikes another two miles up the creek, then crosses it to follow a tributary for a mile to the upper lake. This lake is much larger than the lower one, but its waters are leaner and subject to a more severe climate. Thus its fish, although numerous, do not attain sizes reached by those in the lower lake.

Within Idaho three significant streams (McCoy, Big Elk and Bear creeks) flow into Palisades Reservoir. Having moderate gradients and nutrient rich waters, they are physically similar. Each hosts good populations of cutthroat trout with some individuals attaining large sizes. All are best fished with attractor patterns, are in picturesque settings, and are good mid and late summer walk-in destinations. Before Palisades Dam was created in 1956 these streams also hosted significant runs of spawning cutthroat trout from the Snake. A remnant of this usage remains, particularly in McCoy Creek which also has a colorful history. In the 1870s many of its tributaries hosted eastern Idaho's largest and most notorious gold rush. Only vestiges of this event remain. Tales of Caribou City and Keenan City, located in gold fields on McCoy Creek headwater streams, however, are part of the lore of the old west.

Lower Palisades Lake is a popular destination for anglers and hikers. Located four miles up a well maintained forest service trail from Palisades Campground, it holds cutthroat trout to trophy sizes. Bruce Staples

SALT RIVER DRAINAGE

Salt River flows north out of the beautifully pastoral Star Valley in western Wyoming to empty into the southeast end of Palisades Reservoir. This once pristine stream of varied habitat is now heavily degraded because of siltation brought on by riparian zone destruction through livestock usage. Most major tributaries to the Salt River drain nutrient rich waters from the Caribou and Peale ranges in Idaho's extreme eastern Bonneville and Caribou counties.

In their upper reaches these streams and their tributaries are similar in character—high gradient freestone courses of riffles, pools and runs interspaced by slower stretches winding through meadows. It would be tedious to describe each stream because from Spring Creek in the south to Jackknife Creek in the north there are more than can be fished in a season. This is beaver country and in the upland meadows, for the delight of the contemplative angler, is the ever changing variety of ponds with trout populations ready to be worked like a puzzle. In the more productive ponds one finds cutthroat in abundance with some reaching trophy sizes. The more southerly ponds hold brook trout. The best approach for those who venture here is to locate the ponds on appropriate topographic maps prepared by the United States Geological Survey. Then, if you have the means, the best of these can be pinpointed when viewed from a low flying aircraft. A good candidate for fishing should have a bluish green color which indicates that the pond has enough depth to hold fish through winter, and it should also have well vegetated boundaries which indicate a well maintained dam. If you go to this extreme note potential ponds on your topographic map and then decide which ponds to visit. Chances are good that

you will have them to yourself. Its even quite possible that some ponds will be fished only by you in a season! When you fish these ponds take along a variety of dry and wet flies and don't forget that camera!

In their lower reaches Spring, Tincup and Jacknife creeks remain moderate gradient streams with riffles, runs and pools holding small cutthroat which will take almost any small pattern offered. The lower reaches of Sage, Crow, Stump and Tygee creeks in Idaho are much different, however, and present different opportunities for the experienced fly fisher. In addition to resident native cutthroat, one finds a population of juvenile and occasional adult brown trout in these now lower gradient meadow streams. Throughout the riffles, glides and pools in these meadows is a rich, seasonably available variety of aquatic insects—from giant and golden stoneflies to caddisflies, mayflies and midges. Terrestrial insects are available from early summer until early autumn, when frosts come to these lovely upland valleys. Throughout the meadows on both streams and their lower tributaries are riffles with the proper gravel substrate, current and oxygen availability for successful spawning. Historically, the native fine spotted and large spotted Snake River cutthroat reared here in good numbers. The water quality is so good that the state of Wyoming operates a hatchery on Webster Creek, a tributary of lower Stump Creek in Idaho, for the purpose of preserving and planting the native fine spotted Snake River cutthroat. On nearby Little Spring Creek a private trout ranch has been established where one can fish, for a fee, for rainbow trout ranging up to enormous sizes. For several decades a run of brown trout, some of enormous size, has migrated

A four-pound brown from the Salt River adds a challenge to fishing Crow Creek. Bruce Staples

Autumn run-up browns from the Salt River come to spawn in choice gravels of the beautiful Crow and Stump creek drainages. These waters also serve as havens for young browns. Many of these fish return to inhabit the Salt River while a few remain to inhabit the choicest spots in the drainages. Jimmy Gabettas

upstream in the fall from Salt River to spawn in the riffles of Crow and Stump creeks as well as their major tributaries. By day these migrants seek cover in the deeper holes and runs. At dusk they move into riffles to conduct their age old rites until the direct light of the following day. Fishing these browns is much like stalking big game with a bow. To be successful one must be as inconspicuous as possible and make perfect presentations with the right patterns. The wrong movement will trigger these cautious game fish into headlong flight from riffles to the deepest cover available. A careless approach by an inexperienced angler provides most of these browns enough warning to retreat to cover long before the hapless soul is within fishing distance. Sharpen your skills before you come here expecting success, and also be aware that there is private land in these meadows. With well honed fishing skills and a courteous approach to landowners you will be in for some very unusual and challenging fly fishing: stalking large, cautious fish in small waters.

Stump Creek not only offers beaver pond spangled meadows but a rich history. The old Lander Cutoff which carried 19th century settlers to Oregon and California follows it course! The Oneida Salt works, a vital concern in those days was also sited on Stump Creek. Bruce Staples

WILLOW CREEK DRAINAGE

Within the highlands a few miles to the southeast of Idaho Falls is an entire drainage system that is much overlooked by fly fishers because of the presence of more storied adjacent waters. This is the Willow Creek drainage which has more surface area than some of the other rivers discussed in this overview. None of the streams exceed a few dozen cubic feet per second in their base flows, and many are degraded by siltation brought on by poor agricultural and livestock practices. Stream quality has been lowered so much in many areas that there are only remnants of a once good population of giant and golden stoneflies. One stream, in fact, has had its entire reach dewatered by two-thirds its volume to satisfy water rights in another drainage. The historic inhabitants of this drainage are cutthroat trout. To supplement this dwindling native stock the Idaho Department of Fish and Game started releasing quantities of brook, brown, rainbow and cutthroat trout throughout the drainage in the 1960s. They are all doing well and run to trophy size in the rich waters. Included in this population are brown trout that exceed 10 pounds. Why is this degraded drainage of small streams so productive? Stream gradients are usually moderate, waters are rich with nutrients, ground water recharge is usually reliable, and some good spawning areas are present. But the crucial reason is the large amount of cover in the form of beaver ponds. These ponds provide shelter to trout for surviving severe winters and are always a safe haven from predators as well as supplying an almost unequaled variety of food forms. Beavers create most of the quality fisheries in this drainage and also decide their future.

The two main forks of the Willow Creek system (Willow Creek proper and Gray's Lake Outlet) merge in a canyon in the highlands of Bonneville County to form the lower reach of Willow Creek. Ririe Reservoir is below this confluence and provides warm water species and some trout mainly for anglers with boats or float tubes. Most of the highly productive waters in the drainage are above this confluence, so we will look at this area more closely.

Willow Creek proper and Cranes Creek originate from springs and small headwater streams on the western edge of Willow Creek Lava Field in eastern Bingham County. In its upper reaches Willow Creek is enhanced by streams and springs emanating in the eastern slopes of the Blackfoot Range and in the lava field itself. The streams flow at generally low gradients in willow lined bottoms flanked by benches with rich groves of quaking aspen. This is ideal beaver country and has resulted in a self-sustaining fishery approachable to the walk-in fisherman over private and public lands. Gaining access to streams is a growing problem and is the result of years of private property being vandalized. Posted land is common and many landowners refuse with open hostility any request to access streams on their land. Ranchers and farmers, often living far from their property and livelihood, have to deal with livestock being injured or killed by gunshot, machinery and buildings riddled

Facing page: *Beaver ponds supply habitat throughout Willow Creek drainage that produces large brook, cutthroat, and brown trout ranging to double figure poundage. Bruce Staples*

Grays Lake in early autumn. The huge marsh in eastern Bonneville Country holds a vital federal refuge for wildlife and migratory birds. A whooping crane restoration experiment is in progress here. From the marsh to the northwest flows Gray's Lake Outlet, producer of large brown and cutthroat trout. On the east side of the marsh one sees Caribou Mountain, site of a frantic 1870's gold rush. Bruce Staples

Willow creek drainage abounds in beaver ponds and potholes that host magnificent brown, brook and cutthroat trout. Much of the drainage is within an hour's drive of town on the Snake River plain, and thus provides an easily approached alternative to the more crowded Henry's Fork and South Fork of the Snake River drainages. Jimmy Gabettas

Contact! A large brown takes a leech pattern offered in a Willow Creek beaver pond on a late spring evening. Jimmy Gabettas

with bullet holes, gates and fences destroyed, planted fields mangled by passage of vehicles and the accumulation of litter. A number of years ago I stopped one evening on my way home from fishing Homer Creek when I observed a rancher repairing a fence beside the Long Valley road. His reply to my request to access Willow Creek on his land was a stern, emotional warning:

"See that grain field out here, fella? It's mine! Some of you so-called sportsmen think you can go through and tear it up and throw your garbage on it just to go fishing! I don't know how many times I've had to take the loss, pick up your garbage or fix this fence! That's my living out there, and you keep you ass out of it!"

It's not hard to understand this anger and frustration. I feel the same way when garbage is thrown on my lawn or my property is abused. But this situation is so unnecessary. Part of being a sportsman is having respect for property—public and private. It is in our best interest to seek out the landowner and obtain his written permission for passage. In fact this is the law in the state of Idaho. I go even further. I offer landowners who grant me fishing access my card with my address, phone number and vehicle description and registration. I also make it clear that I will inform them of any illegal act I see performed or having taken place on their property, and, on their request, support them in any legal action. These acts have gained me permission for access in some cases, but there are other property owners who will never again grant access and for good reasons. Nevertheless, there are still many places where one can fish the productive beaver ponds and potholes in this drainage. When you go, bring a variety of flies, large and small, wet and dry. There are many life forms available to trout here and it is never certain which will be effective at a given time.

Willow Creek's main tributary from the east drains the expansive marsh known as Gray's Lake. This stream is Gray's Lake

Leaving the Willow Creek lava field southeast of Idaho Falls, Willow Creek cuts an 800-foot deep canyon on its descent to the Snake River plain. Ririe Dam impounds waters for miles in the lower canyon providing fishing for trout and bass just minutes from Idaho Falls. Bruce Staples

Outlet, and it starts as a mere trickle in the northwest corner of the marsh. As it drops into the upper canyon springs supplement its flow so that below the cascades within the canyon its rich waters support insect life and fish on a year-round basis. Below this upper canyon Gray's Lake Outlet flows easily in a long, twisting reach through a meadow. It is joined by Brockman Creek which, in the area known as Duckworth Meadows, holds stairstep beaver ponds inhabited by brown trout ranging up to large sizes as well as native cutthroat trout. In the early season Gray's Lake Outlet appears to be a classic meadow stream with large populations of caddisflies, midges, mayflies and damselflies. Cutthroat and brown trout are present during the early season when water is plentiful. But later in the season, as flows drop to their base level, one returns in mid summer to find the meadows nearly barren of fish—even during years of normal precipitation. The reason is simple. Much of the reach in the meadows is shallow and warms to temperatures that deplete oxygen to levels that are unbearable for trout during daytime hours. This condition is worsened because the thick decaying vegetation also uses oxygen. Thus, after the early season many residents migrate downstream to the canyon where other streams enhance water flows and cool the stream to the point where enough dissolved oxygen is present to support them.

This condition in the meadows has not always existed. Until the 1930s the flow down Gray's Lake Outlet was about three times its present volume. Then water was diverted out of the southwest end of Gray's Lake through Clark's Cut to Meadow Creek which empties into Blackfoot Reservoir. This action was performed to fulfill downstream irrigation water rights, but it lowered the flow in the outlet and caused the loss of a fabulous cutthroat trout fishery.

Perhaps only part of the tales about potato sacks filled with cutthroat in excess of two pounds in a day's fishing in the meadows are true. Nevertheless, we have lost an unusually productive fishery. In the autumn of 1976 the Idaho Department of Fish and Game chemically treated the entire reach of Gray's Lake Outlet from its cascades in the upper canyon to its confluence with Willow Creek in the lower canyon. This action was performed to eradicate the Utah chub which had been released by bait fishermen and subsequently over-populated the meadows and greatly reduced the trout population. Huge numbers of chubs were killed before the stream was restocked with cutthroat and brown trout. Only a few trout were known to inhabit the meadows at that time. They were killed by the poisoning but among their numbers were brown trout ranging up to 29 inches in length!

In the canyon below the meadows Gray's Lake Outlet is joined by a number of streams that contain their own excellent fisheries enhanced by the presence of beaver ponds. Of these Lava Creek supports a spawning run of cutthroat trout and rears a cutthroat population, as does Homer Creek which also holds brook and brown trout in almost unequaled nutrient rich waters. These streams improve the Outlet's fishery in the canyon, but there are few places where it can be reached because of its deep and difficult nature. Where it can be reached, in such places as Horse Creek Road or from Jumpoff Hill jeep trail, it provides excellent fishing worthy, in normal water years, of the effort required to access it. As with other streams in this area always carry a wide variety of flies. There is a rich assortment of food forms available to trout in these isolated waters, but little information is available on what they will be feeding on at any given time.

BLACKFOOT RIVER DRAINAGE

The Blackfoot River originates from numerous springs and streams in the Webster Range, Dry Ridge and Rassmussen Ridge, all part of the Peale Range. These sources combine to form south flowing Lanes Creek and north flowing Diamond Creek. Each flows several miles to merge almost in the middle of the unique and exquisitely beautiful Upper Valley. This confluence forms the Blackfoot River and the huge meadow surrounding it has been private land for most of the twentieth century. The Stocking family homesteaded the meadow from the confluence of Lanes and Diamond creeks downstream to near the top of the Upper Narrows in 1907. They still own the land and for over three quarters of a century have used it to raise livestock. The river flows more than four miles through their land and is a classic meadow stream reminiscent in form to Slough Creek or the Bechler River in Yellowstone National Park.

There is a major difference between the Blackfoot River and the meadow streams of Yellowstone. The underlying rock beneath most of the Blackfoot River and its drainage readily gives up minerals to make the river waters rich in nutrients for building a diverse food chain. Thus native cutthroat and occasional brook trout moving down from beaver ponds on Diamond Creek have prospered by feeding on the great abundance of aquatic insects and living in the cover of deep holes in each bend of the slow moving stream. This lovely area has the look and feel of a sanctuary for cutthroat trout and it should— residents can grow to several pounds.

The springtime spawning run from the reservoir migrates through to reach the gravels of headwater streams. This run lasts well into June in years of normal water levels. To protect spawners the headwaters downstream to the upper narrows are closed to fishing until the first day in July. By this time thick mayfly and caddisfly emergences are going on in the meadows of the Upper Valley and terrestrial insect populations are building. Stream siltation from decades of livestock grazing is a growing concern in the Upper Valley, but is reversible, and as we shall see in a few paragraphs, not the major problem facing the fishery. Below the Stocking property the river enters Caribou National Forest and flows for about three

Blackfoot River at the top of the Lower Narrows. Below is the short, steep canyon, then a lower gradient reach. The combined waters produce one of the densest giant stonefly populations anywhere. Consequently trout grow easily to trophy sizes here and many move to the reservoir below. Bruce Staples

miles through the Upper Narrows where more tributaries join it. Good populations of giant and golden stoneflies are present to provide plenty of trout food.

Below the Upper Narrows the Blackfoot River enters, appropriately, the Lower Valley. In this area it becomes more of a riffle and pool stream with deep holes and areas of thick willows. Phosphate mining activities are ongoing in the hills surrounding this area but the effects on the fishery are not yet defined. Nevertheless, these effects of mining should be monitored by fisheries managers because of the potential of chemical changes that might destroy entire populations of aquatic life forms.

Other causes of degradation are more obvious. At the upper end of the Lower Valley a large irrigation diversion dewaters the river to a point where significant numbers of fry and adult fish are taken directly from the stream. In places even willows have been eradicated resulting in riparian zone destruction. This has resulted in siltation of the entire reach of the river and diminished numbers of fish. At the lower end of the valley the river drops into the Lower Narrows and changes character. Runs, pocket water and rapids bordering on cascades are interspersed with deep holes. Caddisflies and giant and golden stoneflies abound in densities equal to those found in Box and Cardiac canyons of Henry's Fork. Some very large cutthroat trout reside here in an environment that is somewhat isolated and reachable only by long walks through private land. Below, the river breaks out onto a flat where it has been much degraded by a 50 year old channel alteration and riparian zone destruction. After the flat the stream is confined to a small canyon and eventually empties into the Blackfoot Reservoir—which inundates vast marshes and hay fields.

The dam was finished in 1909 to provide irrigation water for agricultural activities in the Snake River Plain. It also provided habitat in which the native cutthroat trout thrived. But something has gone wrong with the native trout population in the reservoir and the river above it. Up to the late 1950s the reservoir produced cutthroat up to 15 pounds and, according to Idaho Fish and Game Department records, one year in that decade nearly 15,000 fish

The sculpin inhabits silt free riffles and runs and provides another food for trout. It is an indicator of instream quality. Jimmy Gabettas

were removed from the system with approximately 20 percent of them exceeding 20 inches! This phenomenal number of large fish was only a fraction of the estimated half million cutthroat the reservoir hosted at this time. By the early 1970s the number of large cutthroats taken from the system had dropped to approximately 27 percent greater than 14 inches, still a good number by any standard. By the late 1980s, however, the native cutthroat fishery was in a state of collapse, and angler hours declined to about 1,000 a year on the river above the reservoir. Then a dedicated group of fisheries managers collected information and data on cutthroat in the system. What emerged was enlightening and showed that the

Brook trout were introduced to eastern Idaho waters many decades ago. They now are an important constituent of the local fishery, being found in all water types. In certain lakes, springs, reservoirs and beaver ponds in Camas Creek, Henry's Fork, Big Lost River, Little Lost River, Willow Creek and Salt River drainages they grow to trophy sizes. Jimmy Gabettas

decline was reversible. To begin, the reservoir is a tremendous fish factory. Rough fish populations alone grew so numerous that they have been harvested commercially for pet food. Rainbow trout were introduced into the reservoir in the early 1960s and have become the workhorse game fish, thriving in the reservoir and then spawning in the Lower Narrows. A magnificent story of the native cutthroat life cycle was revealed. In April and May mature cutthroat, at least four years old, would migrate from the reservoir into the river and tributaries to spawn in June. Through the 1950s the reservoir was a sanctuary for them because fishing pressure was relatively light. This meant large numbers of cutthroat ascended the drainage, some going as far as 60 miles into distant tributaries. Many of those that survived to descend the river from July to early September were caught by anglers, but their contribution to the system had been made. Most of their progeny in the drainage would then descend to the reservoir after two or three years to grow to maturity, then ascend the river to spawn thus completing the cycle. By the early 1960s many power boats were being used to fish the reservoir allowing more efficient access. Fishing success for large cutthroats was so good that pressure grew a hundred fold. By the 1980s the native cutthroat population began to collapse.

Much of the solution to bringing back the native cutthroat is to manage the reservoir and river with restrictive bag limits, say the fisheries managers. They are presently examining, with public input and optimism, the options for doing this. They also believe that improvement can be obtained even more quickly if agricultural, water management, mining and livestock practices are changed to favor the fishery. Meanwhile the reservoir is still best fished from boats or float tubes by the fly fisher equipped with streamer and leech patterns, and good catches of mainly rainbow trout can result.

Another shore dweller common throughout eastern Idaho, the egret can be seen in large numbers along Market Lake, American Falls Reservoir and the numerous irrigation reservoirs in Franklin and Oneida counties. Ken Retallic

Yellow-headed black birds are common throughout the marsh and meadow areas in eastern Idaho. Extensive populations are found in preserves such as the Market Lake Wildlife Management Area and the Gray's Lake National Wildlife Refuge. Ken Retallic

A few other facts about the drainage above the reservoir are of interest. Emptying into the reservoir at its northeast corner is Meadow Creek which, in places above its cascades, holds very large cutthroat trout. The Little Blackfoot River also empties into the east end of the reservoir at the townsite of Henry. The Idaho Department of Fish and Game has introduced a Bear Lake strain of cutthroat trout into this smallest of rivers with hope of establishing a population which will reside in the reservoir and then ascend it for spawning.

Until recently the Blackfoot River in the canyon below the dam provided a fishery offering huge individual cutthroat and rainbow trout, many of which were escapees from the reservoir above. Throughout the irrigation season the waters released from the reservoir would fluctuate wildly making fishing success uncertain. As summer progressed and waters in the canyon warmed these fish would migrate to the large holes just below the dam to obtain cover and the vital oxygen concentrations found in the cooler water. This migration resulted in heavy fishing pressure below the dam, but for many years, the numbers of large trout seemed to hold up well. By 1987 the dam was rebuilt and raised and the channel below altered. This action has prevented escape of fish from the reservoir and degraded the river channel just below it. Some fishing for cutthroat and rainbow trout remains in the canyon below the dam and in the Brush Creek drainage contributing to it, but what is left is only a fraction of the once quality fishery of former times.

The story of the whole Blackfoot River drainage is, sadly, that of a diminishing resource. For the reservoir and river above, the future may be good if more emphasis is placed on enhancing or even just maintaining what is left. This will require effort and cooperation by all users: fisheries managers, irrigators, miners, sportsmen and stockmen alike.

PORTNEUF RIVER DRAINAGE

The Portneuf River drains most of the land between the Blackfoot and Bear River drainages. Above Lava Hot Springs this includes the area between the Portneuf Range on the west and the Chesterfield and Fish Creek ranges on the east. Much of this is in the Portneuf Valley through which the river flows to the south and in which are located Chesterfield and Twenty-four Mile reservoirs. Waters in the north end of this valley are on the Fort Hall Indian Reservation and thus subject to tribal regulations.

Just after the turn of the century miles of river channel below Chesterfield Reservoir were straightened for agricultural purposes. Few records remain concerning the quality of the river fishery in the valley before construction of the reservoir. Below the valley the Portneuf turns westerly, upstream from Lava Hot Springs, then north, then northwesterly again to empty into American Falls Reservoir. In this lower reach it drains the west slopes of the Portneuf Range, Marsh Creek and the north slopes of the Bannock Range. In its natural state the river is similar in volume to the Blackfoot River with a variety of gradients, nutrient rich water, good cover, gravel for spawning and fish rearing areas. Like many other highland streams its upper reach is generally of lower gradient. Then, as it passes into its canyon, it is mostly faster water—at times bordering on falls as found around Lava Hot Springs. Downstream as it breaks onto the Snake River Plain its gradient slows again.

Unlike highland drainages such as those producing the Teton, Willow Creek, Salt River and Blackfoot River, the Portneuf does not have an extensive system of tributaries suitable for spawning and rearing. Municipal development from Lava Hot Springs downstream eliminated a once quality cutthroat trout fishery years ago. The reach above Inkom holds some large brown trout, but only a fraction of what could be present with quality habitat conditions. Marsh Creek, the main tributary in this area, has the look of a classic meadow stream but years of overgrazing and dewatering have degraded it terribly. The river below is degraded to an almost lifeless state.

Around 15,000 years ago Marsh Creek Valley and the Portneuf Canyon below Lave Hot Springs hosted the prodigious flood that came from the release of Lake Bonneville to the south. This flood, one of the largest recorded, happened when the lake broke through the present Red Rock Pass near the town of Swanlake and coursed to the Snake River and on to the Pacific Ocean by way of the Columbia River. The remnant of Lake Bonneville is the Great Salt Lake.

As recently as the 1970s Portneuf, above Lava Hot Springs, was a destination fishery for local and out of state anglers. During much of the season Chesterfield and Twenty-four Mile reservoirs would be alive with boat and bank anglers hoping for trophy rainbow and cutthroat trout. Downstream meadows through which the river flowed in pools, riffles and runs produced large quantities of cutthroat and rainbow with good numbers of trophy sized individuals. Now we are losing this fishery at an alarming rate. Draw down to satisfy increased agricultural demands has dewatered the

cold water fisheries in Chesterfield and Twenty-four Mile reservoirs. Continuing erosion by the early century channel alteration below Chesterfield Reservoir added silt to the system. So bleak was the habitat of these once productive reservoirs that they became managed mainly as put and take propositions with the possibility of future conversion to warm water fisheries. The best tributaries for spawning and rearing have been altered to the point of being of little value in enhancing the river. King Creek is highly dewatered before it reaches the river. Toponce Creek is a beautiful headwater stream with a good fishery of brook and native cutthroat trout in its beaver ponds and pockets. It is, however, completely diverted to Chesterfield Reservoir in its lower reach. Pebble Creek still has potential to serve the river, even with the diversion of some of its water. But it is in the river where the biggest loss is ongoing because of extensive and continuing siltation brought on mainly by poor agricultural practices throughout the reach.

Restoration of irrigation reservoirs throughout the Portneuf, Bear and Malad River drainages are paying off in benefits of bass, trout and panfish for float tubers and bank anglers alike. Jimmy Gabettas

Snake River fine spotted as well as Yellowstone cutthroat trout inhabit lakes and streams. This early season female from Chesterfield Reservoir shows the silvery sides and greenish hues common to lake and reservoir residents. Carol Staples

The effects of stream siltation can be devastating because it degrades in so many ways. Vital gravels for spawning and insect production are smothered and holes that provide cover fill in. These actions decrease the average stream depth which warms its waters. Warming of water in turn decreases the amount of oxygen that can dissolve. So the silted stream offers little to the fishery, not only in terms of cover and spawning areas but also in terms of food and, most vital of all, available oxygen. This whole spectrum of degradation is affecting the upper Portneuf and presently little relief is in site.

Perhaps the best place to see what the Portneuf once had to offer is in the meadows above Pebble Creek. Here in some of the riffles, runs and slow meanders where the substrate is not smothered in silt there is a rich variety of aquatic insects including several species each of caddisflies and mayflies. A few species of small stoneflies, leeches, fresh water shrimp, craneflies and midges are also present. There is cover underneath overhangs and below rocks and ledges. There is also depth for added cover and for cooling. But these areas are isolated by large tracts where siltation has smothered all. A good indicator of conditions is that the large stoneflies, once present in large populations, have disappeared because silt free bottoms and dissolved oxygen levels they need no longer exist on a proper scale. Still there are rainbow and brown trout with a few cutthroat in the upper river and a good day's fishing can be had, but with each passing year of ongoing siltation the remnant fishery will decline further.

It is encouraging that certain landowners, fisheries researchers and anglers are recognizing the plight of the Portneuf fishery, and efforts are being made to correct this unnecessary situation. Management of Chesterfield and Twenty-four Mile reservoirs has changed to build trophy cutthroat and rainbow fisheries. Stream fencing projects have been started and a few riparian zones are regaining a foothold. Research is underway to learn more about the fishery but agricultural practices which allow erosion from runoff and subsequent stream siltation must cease if the fishery is to be helped. Adopting these practices will not be easy but the siltation can be stopped and even reversed. This, however, will take time and dedication. In the balance is the loss of a tremendously productive and economically important fishery.

The Portneuf Range glows in the September afternoon sunlight. Below, the river holds cutthroat, rainbow and brown trout to entice the angler. Bruce Staples

BEAR RIVER DRAINAGE

The Bear River originates on the northern slopes of the Uinta Range in Utah and flows in a wide arc through southwestern Wyoming, southeastern Idaho, then back into northern Utah to the Great Salt Lake. Other than the Snake River, the Bear River has the longest reach of any stream in eastern Idaho. In its course through Idaho it drains the Preuss, Wasatch and Bannock ranges.

The much degraded Malad River has an extensive drainage in Idaho southwest of the Bannock Range and flows into the Bear River in Utah. Some of the Malad River's headwater streams still provide good fishing for small trout. The Bear River system is the only one in eastern Idaho that is part of the Great Basin drainage, and it may also be our most abused. Livestock activities have been devastating meadows and riparian zones on the Bear River for over a century. Likewise, siltation and dewatering from poor agricultural practices have clogged its channels throughout. So degraded are its waters that even Alexander and Oneida reservoirs on its reach are managed as warm water or put and take trout fisheries. The operation of hydropower facilities at the dams and seasonal irrigation demand have altered flows from dewatering to flooding for much of the twentieth century. For more than a century the nutrient lean

waters of Bear Lake have been invaded by the nutrient rich runoff waters from Bear River for storage for downstream power generation and irrigation. The effects of this practice on the lake's fishery is yet to be fully assessed. Recent drought and drawdown for agricultural purposes has had a negative effect on the ability of Bear Lake cutthroat to ascend tributary streams for spawning. In the balance little natural reproduction of trout occurs throughout Bear River, thus its once healthy population of native cutthroat trout are but a remnant. Nevertheless there are occasional numbers of brown, cutthroat and rainbow trout in the river and in the Thomas Fork, a major upstream tributary. But these are local, varying and best experienced by those who reside nearby. Sadly there is little to attract the contemplative angler to the Bear River itself when much better fishing is available on adjacent drainages, but certain tributaries do offer fishing worthy of consideration.

In Bear Lake County several tributaries draining out of the Preuss Range to Bear River hold populations of trout in reaches that are not dewatered. Montpelier Creek flows through a steep canyon which holds a reservoir nearly two miles long. Brown, cutthroat and rainbow trout can provide good action when waters are

Twin Lakes, northwest of Preston in Franklin County, is a popular warm water destination for eastern Idaho anglers. Bass, trout and panfish inhabit its waters. In the distance one sees the snow-capped Wasatch Range around which Bear River swings to flow into the Great Salt Lake farther south. Bruce Staples

lower and less variable, particularly in mid and late season. Georgetown Creek also originates in the same mountains and hosts a population of cutthroat and rainbow trout. Preuss Creek to the northeast holds a native cutthroat trout fishery. In the past all these creeks have undergone hatchery planting to sustain their fisheries. On the other side of Bear River Valley, Saint Charles Creek provides spawning and rearing habitat for the Bear Lake strain of cutthroat. Several creeks draining the Wasatch Range, from Bloomington Creek on the south to Eight-mile Creek on the north, hold cutthroat and sometimes rainbow trout populations. Big and beautiful Bear Lake contains cutthroat which sometimes attain weights close to 20 pounds, and a good population of lake trout was established about 50 years ago. The Bear Lake strain of cutthroat are particularly valuable being a diminishing sub species of the Bonneville cutthroat. But these fish are available mainly to the fly fisher equipped with streamer flies and a boat or float tube. The best chance for action for one so equipped is in front of creeks, mainly the Little Creek branch of Saint Charles Creek, early in the summer when the cutthroats return to the lake from their spawning runs or October and November in shallower waters when the lake trout spawn.

Where Bear River flows through southeastern Caribou County near the town of Grace, brown, cutthroat and rainbow trout are found in Black Canyon, and holdovers reach large sizes. In Franklin County potentially good habitat is found below Oneida Reservoir. Power peaking from the dam varies flows from under 100 to over 2,000 cubic feet per second! This devastates the stream habitat, and because these variations can occur daily no single fishing strategy is entirely effective.

In this area both Mink Creek and Cub River, flowing from the Wasatch Range to the east, formerly hosted spawning runs of brown and cutthroat trout. Now these tributaries are dewatered and diverted to the point where they cannot be used for this purpose by river fish. Farther up in the mountains these streams still hold populations of small trout. But because of siltation, fluctuations in flow and destruction of spawning habitat the fishery in the river below is presently in a state of collapse. Now the main attraction in the area is the spiny ray fisheries of bass, crappie and bluegill which have been established in the local reservoirs. These offer an early season release for the fly fisher awaiting the end of runoff, and

The Bear Lake strain are among the most beautiful of cutthroat trout. Programs are underway to restore this treasure in Bear Lake and to introduce it to other appropriate waters in the Bear River and Blackfoot River drainages. Courtesy of Richard Dorfman and Steve Elle, Idaho Department of Fish and Game

for some anglers these fisheries have even become a destination. Wet attractor patterns are fare of the day. Streamers and patterns that simulate leeches, damselfly nymphs, mayfly emergers and even nothing in particular are effective.

Nearly two dozen of these reservoirs, all of which function to supply water for agricultural purposes, are found in this area which encompasses parts of Bannock, Caribou, Franklin and Oneida counties. Some are worthy of mention because they have offered consistently good fishing for non-native species. Condie Reservoir, a few miles south of Treasureton produces largemouth bass up to eight pounds. Nearby Treasureton Reservoir has produced largemouth to four pounds. Twin Lakes near Clifton, the largest impoundment in the area, has many game fish species but also has a prolific (good weather) emergence of boaters and water skiers. In past years Daniels Reservoir, northwest of Malad, produced holdover rainbow trout growing to several pounds, but the release of rough fish all but exterminated them by the 1980s. Presently Idaho Department of Fish and Game is attempting to restore the trout population in this reservoir, and they appear to be succeeding.

On the whole the quality of fishing in these reservoirs varies depending on water demands, winter kills and introduction of rough fish. So it is best to check with local sporting good dealers, fisheries managers or knowledgeable anglers to obtain information about which are currently producing good fishing.

The Black Canyon of the Bear River above the Grace Power Plant is still an angler destination for good rainbow and cutthroat trout. Efforts to return parts of habitat to natural conditions could make Bear River again a high quality fishery. Bruce Staples

SINKS DRAINAGES

Volcanism created a unique and dominant landform in eastern Idaho called the Snake River Plain. The Snake River flows southwesterly through this stark and arid geographic feature and is joined at intervals by tributaries from highlands to the east. A look at a road map, however, shows that streams originating in the mountains to the north never reach the river; they end on the plain. The same volcanism which has occurred as recently as a few thousand years ago created the sinks drainages. The geologic story of the phenomenon is fascinating, but too long and irrelevant other than to briefly outline.

It appears that as few as 10,000 years ago the ancestral Snake River flowed west from present Menan Buttes through the Market Lake/Mud Lake area. From here it skirted the southern edge of the Lemhi, Lost River and Pioneer ranges on its westerly course. Most likely when it was in this course streams from mountains to the north were in its drainage as, in some manner, were those coming from the highlands to the east. Then, with volcanism and southward moving lava flows, the Snake River downstream of

Menan Buttes was slowly pushed to its current path through southeast and southcentral Idaho. At or near this time broad uplift north of the plain caused Birch Creek and the Lost Rivers to flow in the direction of the Salmon River. With more recent geologic subsidence and retreat of glaciation these streams flowed again in the direction of the Snake River, displaced far to the south. At the time of their return, however, they were blocked from access to the river by higher lands to the south. Near the edge of the plain their nutrient rich waters pooled, and the water that did not evaporate in the dry desert air sank through the lavas to recharge the aquifer below. The sinks drainages consist of streams that, with exception of the Big Lost River, are each less than 100 cubic feet per second in base flow. Scenic mountain lakes are also present in most of these drainages. Originally some contained no trout and others were inhabited by native cutthroat or perhaps rainbow trout. Now brook, brown, rainbow and cutthroat are present in sustaining and abundant populations and in many locations grow to trophy sizes.

CAMAS CREEK DRAINAGE

Camas Creek drains the area immediately west of Island Park; of all the sinks drainages it is the easiest to visualize as a tributary to the Snake River. Except for its ending it is similar in form to the highland drainages to the southeast. Its network of headwater streams drain the Centennial Range, then collect in an upland valley to form the mainstem. From here the mainstem flows through a canyon which at one time may have emptied into the ancestral Snake River but which now flows into Mud Lake.

The jewel of the drainage is Aldous Lake in the foothills of the Centennials just off Ching Creek. After a one mile walk up its outlet creek (located at the end of the Ching Creek Road) one can see this nearly oval lake of only a few hundred yards in length. On closer observation cutthroat trout up to trophy sizes can be seen cruising the shorelines. A float tube is necessary to obtain a position to cast damselfly patterns, leeches, or speckled dun imitations to these cruisers because the lake shore is either forested or too steep to permit a back cast.

The streams converging to form Camas Creek are known for their populations of eager brook trout. Requests for access along the streams are usually granted by landowners, and the result is hours of nonstop action by brookies that will take almost any offering. Where Camas Creek drops into its canyon, almost at the Red Road crossing, it becomes a different stream in character and inhabitants. Brown trout, some large, dominate the canyon waters. Their numbers vary with water conditions, and recent drought years have taken their toll. To the west Beaver Creek drains the Idaho side of Monida Pass. The stream's reach above the town of Spencer is a superb high country fishery holding brook, cutthroat and rainbow trout all of which attain surprising sizes. Best numbers of trout are

found in the canyon just off the interstate highway a few miles above Spencer. Access to the mouth of the canyon is easily obtained just off the highway, and one can walk up the railroad line to approach the lightly fished pockets, potholes and beaver ponds where almost any fly of small or medium size will be taken.

A chance for a trophy cutthroat trout is the reward for the angler who carries his float tube to Aldous Lake in the Centennial Range above the Kilgore ranching community. This spring-fed lake contributes water to Camas Creek, the first drainage west of the Henry's Fork. Bruce Staples

Downstream on the Snake River Plain Beaver and Camas creeks combine, but because of diversion for agriculture water flows only during runoff. The dewatered creek courses to Mud Lake. Until just after the turn of the century this large seepage lake hosted a healthy cutthroat trout population which spawned during spring in the creek above the lake. At that time the bottom and shore line of the lake were free of silt, and its waters were not consumed for agricultural use. Today agricultural wells have depleted the water table which supplies the lake and its springs and this, combined with diversion of surface waters to the surrounding desert for agricultural purposes, has shallowed the lake. Silt from adjacent agricultural practices has invaded its shores, and the lake is no longer capable of sustaining a cold water fishery. Thus it is currently managed for spiny ray fish, particularly predators such as the tiger muskie which prey on the abundant rough fish population.

MEDICINE LODGE CREEK DRAINAGE

One of the more remote fisheries in eastern Idaho is Medicine Lodge Creek. Its headwaters start in the southeast slopes of the Beaverhead Range, then unite to form the stream which runs through a series of scenic upland meadows. On its course to the southeast Medicine Lodge Creek appears to flow towards Beaver Creek to become part of the Camas Creek drainage. But after it exits a brief canyon just below the meadows to enter the Snake River Plain it turns south near the townsite of Small. Downstream from here what is left of it, after diversion for irrigation, gradually sinks into the lava beds.

Where it courses through hay meadows above the plain it is a classic meadow stream with deep undercuts, overhanging cover, riffles and pools. These meadows are mostly private lands but many owners grant permission to access the stream. What awaits the angler is surprising and rewarding: not only a few eager cutthroat

trout, but rainbows up to trophy size. Dry and wet attractor and terrestrial patterns in small and medium sizes used from early summer to mid autumn will always produce action. Catching the larger rainbows certainly requires skill, but action aplenty is supplied by the smaller trout throughout the meadows and in the faster sections of the creek and its tributaries. In passing it is interesting to note that Divide Lake at the head of the drainage was once planted with grayling. These remained for a time but have disappeared, perhaps succumbing to a winter kill. Now this lake hosts a healthy population of cutthroat trout.

Mule deer are native to eastern Idaho. They are frequent visitors to streams and lakes, and their sightings add quality to the angling experience. In the ranching country on Medicine Lodge Creek they frequent the meadowed stream bottoms year round, but retreat to the timbered benches when danger is sensed. Doug Wenzel

Smaller streams of the sinks drainages provide an escape from the heralded waters of the area. Streams such as Medicine Lodge Creek, Camas Creek and Little Lost River provide opportunities to answer the sound of small waters. Jimmy Gabettas

BIRCH CREEK DRAINAGE

Birch Creek flows from tributaries in the Beaverhead and Lemhi mountain ranges and from springs on the south side of Gilmore Summit. Through almost its entire course it is a moderate gradient, freestone stream comprised of riffles, runs and pocket water in series. Wild brook and rainbow trout inhabit its upper reaches. Stocked rainbow trout dominate the reach from the upper State Highway 28 crossing downstream and holdovers occasionally reach surprising size.

Birch Creek has a base flow of less than 100 cubic feet per second. It is of immense value (and would be to any area), for it is the quintessential family stream having introduced a large number of youngsters to the joys of angling. When travelling State Highway 28 between the Snake River Plain and Gilmore Summit during summer one always sees a line of recreation vehicles parked in the creek's riparian zone. It doesn't matter that most of the rainbows are planted or what the terminal gear or attention spans are. What is priceless is the sheer joy and satisfaction that the neophyte angler experiences. Lifetimes of enjoyment begin on streams like Birch Creek, and many seasoned eastern Idaho anglers fondly recall their early experiences here.

The mainly put-and-take fishery of Birch Creek provides action and experience for younger and tyro anglers. Each season the population of hatchery-reared rainbows is supplemented by the Idaho Department of Fish and Game, but upper reaches hold sustaining populations of rainbow and brook trout. Jimmy Gabettas

LITTLE LOST RIVER DRAINAGE

Little Lost River drains the valley between the Lemhi Mountain Range to the northeast and the Lost River Range to the southwest. They are Idaho's loftiest mountains and perhaps her driest. Because of this the "Little Lost," as it is known locally, flows mostly through stark, arid land. In its lower reach it is dewatered for irrigation and thus is usually dry long before its sinks are reached south of the town of Howe. The best sustaining trout populations are found in its upper reaches above the Clyde township vicinity. A few miles above Clyde the Little Lost divides into Summit Creek on the west and Sawmill Creek on the east. This is remote mountain country and both creeks drain the divide opposite the Salmon River drainage. In Sawmill Creek, flowing from the north to the Little Lost, also in Wet Creek and Summet Creek is a unique and

The upper Little Lost River drainage provides smaller waters in abundance in a truly remote setting. The presence of rainbow, brook and bull trout make a scenic and interesting trip for the angler seeking small streams. Jimmy Gabettas

fascinating hint of the not too distant past: the only native population of bull trout in eastern Idaho. This presence supports the geologic evidence that in the past the Little Lost, at least in part, was in the Salmon River Drainage, which also hosts bull trout. Other residents include brook and rainbow trout. All three species have individuals growing to surprisingly large size in Sawmill Creek and Little Lost River.

All of these streams have holes, pockets and riffles in riparian zones. They are a pleasure to fish with light tackle. Wet and dry attractor patterns are fare of the day here, and one never knows when a large brook, bull or rainbow trout will leave its cover to take a presentation. Frequently, however, one is distracted to view the panorama of the sagebrush carpeted valley and slopes and snow splashed rocky peaks above the fringe of forests. To the northeast, in the Lemhis above the Fairview Guard Station on Sawmill Creek, one can walk a few miles up to Mill Creek Lake to find small but eager cutthroat and vistas that will not fade from memory. To the west, on the Lost River Range, Swauger Lakes hold respectable trout. The headwaters of the Little Lost River are truly another example of the best that eastern Idaho offers the angler: quality fishing and relative solitude in country of unparalleled scenic splendor.

BIG LOST RIVER DRAINAGE

If the Big Lost River drainage were almost anywhere but in eastern Idaho it would be a fishery of national renown. In its natural state it offers trout in abundance in every fresh water type except large lakes and rivers. Its sources in the Pioneer, White Knob and Boulder mountains have high mountain lakes (made fishable by the Idaho Department of Fish and Game's successful aerial stocking program) and a vast network of fishable headwater streams. The gem of its sources has to be Copper Basin, named for mining activities which in the late nineteenth century tapped copper, lead and zinc deposits. Only shafts and head frames remain. Above these remnants is the source of the East Fork of the Big Lost

Airplane Lake, also called Wildhorse Lake, has alpine surroundings typical of the numerous lakes in the Big Lost River drainage. Some lakes contain self-sustaining trout populations, others are maintained by the Idaho Department of Fish and Game's aerial stocking program. Situated at elevations around nine to ten thousand feet means these lakes are fishable only three to four months of the year. Ice-out commonly comes by July and freeze-up about the end of October. Ron Mizia

River, an excellent small river holding rainbow and brook trout. Higher up and rimmed by the Pioneer and White Knob ranges are Lake Creek Lakes that, depending on aerial stockings, can hold rainbow, cutthroat or golden trout. At the northwest end of the basin the East Fork is joined by Starhope Creek, also known as the West Fork of the Big Lost River. Lake Creek Lakes and Bellas Lakes add their waters to Starhope Creek. Broad Canyon contains Goat, Betty and Baptie lakes which all hold trout populations and also contribute waters to Starhope. Occasional cutthroat venture down from these lakes to add variety to the streams below. Farther downstream beautiful Wildhorse Creek adds its waters to the East Fork. Its sources hold fishable lakes such as Boulder, Moose, Angel and Arrowhead—a real challenge to reach. As with Lake Creek and Bellas the aerial stocking program has made rainbow and cutthroat trout a staple here, and trophy size individuals are a possibility. In some places such as Bellas Lake one will even find natural reproduction because of the presence of an inlet stream with spawning habitat. However, successful fishing in these lakes is always subject to chance because of winter kills and stocking frequency.

The best advice on fishing the lakes includes contacting the Idaho Department of Fish and Game to obtain information about which lakes have recently been stocked and in which lakes populations of trout are known to exist. Next obtain U.S. Geologic Survey topographic maps of the area. Study them to obtain insight as to the effort and resources needed to reach the fishable lakes,

then make your selection. With respect to flies, fare of the day must be attractor patterns. Certain patterns work better on some lakes than others. This means flashy streamers, nymphs and leeches in small and medium sizes. Dry attractor patterns, particularly those made with peacock herl like the Royal Coachman, Royal Renegade or Gray Hackle Peacock are good general selections. But always take a variety because fish in high mountain lakes are unpredictable. Their behavior can range from greedy to particular to unresponsive. Also keep in mind that the scenery at all the lakes is unparalleled, making a forgotten camera almost a tragedy.

There are more mountain lakes in the drainage of the North Fork of the Big Lost River. This branch drains the Boulder mountains to the west, and in its drainage one finds good populations of brook and rainbow trout as well as some cutthroat. At the head of Antelope Creek, which drains to the lower river, one finds Iron Bog, Fishpole and Brockie lakes, all of which can hold rainbow and cutthroat trout to trophy size.

Where the North and East Forks join just north of Copper Basin the "Big Lost" proper starts. From here downstream in its northeasterly course it is paralleled by Trail Creek Road, making it easily accessible in mostly public land. Here it is a medium gradient upland river with nutrient rich waters and a good population of aquatic insects. Thus attractor patterns, wet or dry, will produce well. Occasional trophies are caught from the predominantly rainbow trout population.

Evidence of the Big Lost's history can be found in this reach. Some of the geologic features lend credibility to the possibility that in the past it could have swung north through Thousand Springs Valley, at the base of Mount Borah, then on through Willow Creek Summit to join the Salmon River near the town of Challis. No definite clues to the past can be found in the trout populations, however. Brook and golden trout are obviously exotic, but records of rainbow and cutthroat stockings are incomplete. So the romantic who suggests that rainbow, in particular, could be a remnant of anadromous Salmon River strains cannot be proven wrong. There is also the fascinating presence of whitefish and sculpin species common to the Salmon River drainage but not to the Snake River drainage. All these facts do not rule out other possibilities. The Big Lost system may have been devoid of trout or it may have contained Snake River cutthroats, which for some unknown reasons did not survive to present times. So the puzzle of the past remains to be discussed and enjoyed.

The East Fork of the Big Lost River is the trunk stream of Copper Basin. Here in its upper reaches are riffles, pools and runs holding an abundance of small but scrappy brook and rainbow trout. Dennis Bitton

Presently the Big Lost makes an arc in the area of Bartlett Point, a spur of the White Knob mountains, and then flows southeast through the Big Lost River Valley. Here it is joined by the outlet of Chilly Sloughs, the major water body in Thousand Springs Valley. The sloughs deserve mention because they host brook trout to trophy size. Fishing them, however, requires three minimum items: land owner permission, a good sense of direction and a boat or canoe. Other spring creeks add nutrient rich waters to the river in the upper end of Big Lost River Valley. Here it is of moderate size and of lower gradient with a somewhat braided channel. Down to Mackay Reservoir its waters and those of adjoining streams still hold a rainbow trout population that is second to none. Trophy sized individuals are common. As in nearly all eastern Idaho valleys much of the water flows through private land, and it is always best to obtain permission to cross such land to access the streams. Mackay Reservoir is surrounded mostly by public land except on its upper end where channels of the Big Lost and other creeks enter it. The reservoir can be fished by casting streamers and leech patterns, particularly in front of the channels at the upper end during summer and autumn. At these times there is always a chance of an exhilarating encounter with a trophy specimen of the predominantly rainbow trout population.

Below Mackay Reservoir the Big Lost flows southeasterly towards the Snake River Plain below the town of Arco. In the past this reach also contributed to the Big Lost's reputation as one of Idaho's most productive trout fisheries. Now the negative impacts of diversion, siltation and water table lowering, particularly below the town of Mackay, have left us with a remnant.

For decades, until the 1950s, the river below Mackay Dam was relatively unexploited and contained a rich population of rainbow and brook trout. Rainbow up to several pounds were frequently caught in the river and in some adjoining spring creeks. Vast tracts of willows protected the stream, and seemingly unlimited numbers of aquatic insects were present. The Big Lost remained in the background as Silver Creek, Henry's Fork and Henry's Lake remained the stars of the Idaho show. Water diversion for irrigation, bank erosion by livestock and channel alteration for flood control were ongoing but did not seem to effect the fishery to a great degree. Fisheries managers warned of potential dangers and noted

Kane Lake is at the head of Kane Creek in the North Fork of the Big Lost River drainage. The long uphill walk is rewarded by eager trout and matchless scenery. Robert Schindler

some decline but the high quality fishery remained. Beginning in the 1950s, however, large numbers of wells were sunk in the lower valley to tap the aquifer and thus provide water for expanding agricultural purposes. Flows in the river began ebbing in years of low rainfall but seemed to rebound in years of water abundance. By the 1980s the wells numbered in the hundreds and flows in the river and adjacent spring creeks were decreased as the water table dropped. This spelled disaster for the quality fishery and trout numbers and size diminished. Where once good fishing could be experienced continuously through the hay meadows south of Arco and into the box canyon at the entry to the Snake River Plain, the river was reduced to intermittent flows. The same condition exists now on the river above Arco and seems to be moving upstream. So the choice has been made between quality fishery and expanded ground water use in the agriculturally based economy below Mackay. Good fishing on a local basis can still be found in the lower valley but it is a remnant which unfortunately will diminish further as more wells tap the aquifer below or during low snowfall years.

Contributing runoff waters to the Big Lost River drainage on the south and west and to the Little Lost River drainage on the north and east, this is Idaho's loftiest mountain range. Few mountain lakes support trout here, but Copper Basin just to the southwest has dozens that do. Marv Hoyt

PART II

FLY PATTERNS

Photography by Jim Schollmeyer

ABOUT THE FLIES

Most books that describe fly patterns contain excellent "how to tie" information but they provide the reader little information with respect to usage. This lack of "how to use" information may be of little concern to the expert fly fisher or to the person interested mainly in the art of fly tying, but for the majority of fly fishers at least some usage information is helpful in making choices of flies for specific water types. In the preceding overview of area waters there is general information about the life forms available to trout in each drainage. In the section that follows on popular flies there is additional information and, where I believe appropriate, specific information. By specific information I mean that a certain pattern simulates a specific insect which is available as a food form to trout at a specific time or in a specific water location. My intent in doing this is to provide the fly fisher with information for making an essential fly selection but not to deter him from experimenting with pattern usage on his own terms. Experimentation leads to discovery which is one of the joys in fly fishing.

You will notice that many of the flies presented, dry or wet, can be considered attractor patterns. There is good reason for this. Attractor patterns are always effective on smaller streams, and east Idaho has an abundance of these with moderate and higher gradients. Eastern Idaho also has an abundance of moderate and higher gradient areas in larger streams. Attractor patterns are always effective in these areas. A large variety of life forms are available to trout in eastern Idaho waters. For example, leeches and minnows are always present in lakes, ponds and slow moving streams. Superimpose dragonfly, damselfly or cranefly emergences, and the right attractor pattern can be taken for any of these by opportunistic feeding trout.

Beyond a few well known individuals there is a relatively unheralded but extensive fly tying tradition in eastern Idaho. Here one finds a spectrum of tiers who have created flies that range from inland steelhead and salmon patterns to warm water patterns and, of course, all types of patterns for trout which exhibit the richest variety because of the abundance of caddisfly, mayfly, stonefly and terrestrial food forms to imitate.

Tiers of trout patterns are specialists in all types of operations such as weaving, extended bodies and hollow hair use. There are specialists in using synthetics and native materials, tying patterns for particular water types and in tying patterns for a particular stream or lake. There are dry fly and wet fly specialists, specialists in hackling and winging, and in not hackling or winging. In short nearly every fly tying specialty is performed in eastern Idaho, and popular patterns from each of these types will be found in this book. In a sense this variety of native fly tiers and their creations compliments the wide variety of area waters. This book begins the process of revealing the eastern Idaho fly tying tradition that has evolved over several decades and is as rich as any found around the waters of this world.

Some of the patterns described require a certain amount of skill to tie. If you need more information to tie specific patterns I suggest acquiring the two superbly illustrated volumes of the *Western Fly Tying Manual* by Jack Dennis. The tying sequence for several of the patterns I describe are photographed in these excellent books. The best approach to sharpening your tying skills, however, is to enroll in fly tying classes. Broad-based fly fishing clubs and quality fly fishing shops offer fly tying classes for beginners as well as advanced tiers. Those instructing the classes are typically fly fishers with a depth of experience in their locality and thus are best qualified to conduct such courses. From these individuals you should not only be able to obtain fly tying skills, but solid and practical information on usage of the patterns tied. If you enjoy fly tying consider that it can become consuming to the point that creating effective or even artistic flies becomes a pursuit for its own sake. In any case fly tying enriches fly fishing, and the sense of accomplishment gained from tying flies that catch fish is one of the most satisfying gifts in all of fishing.

Ardell Jeppsen's Super Renegade has as many variations as the South Fork of the Snake River has water types. The "Super", as it is known locally, is probably the overall most popular wet attractor used by float fishing anglers on the South Fork. The number of variations is a good measure of its effectiveness. Jimmy Gabettas

DRY FLIES

BLOND HUMPY

Hook: *Mustad 7957B, 3906 or equivalent, sizes 8-16.*
Thread: *Yellow monocord, 3/0.*
Tail: *Several hairs from dark brown moose or elk stocking.*

Shellback and Wings: *Formed from bunch of light straw elk rump hair with tips forming wing, upright and divided.*
Hackle: *Two ginger.*

Dan Bailey gets most of the credit for originating this major modification of the Humpy, and when one considers the principle material from which it is made there is little question that it is of western origin. As with the Humpy, however, there are others in the western United States and in Canada's western provinces who claim at least a share of its origin.

The Blond Humpy loses none of the effectiveness of its forebearer and is distinguished by its wings and shellback which are formed of either straw colored elk rump hair, as originally conceived, or bleached elk or deer body hair. The Blond Humpy is another superb attractor pattern for use on higher gradient streams. Sizes 10 through 14 simulate caddisflies, smaller stoneflies and even hoppers in water types where many fly fishers prefer the new version over the original because it is easier to see. I have used it successfully on slower waters with silty bottoms to simulate brown drakes, which emerge in early summer, and gray drakes, which emerge from the same waters in early autumn. This requires the use of a long, fine leader, drag free floats of long distances and a careful approach. The rewards can be strikes by large trout. Try using the Blond Humpy during these emergences in areas such as the meadow sections of the Blackfoot River, Willow Creek or the spring creeks above American Falls Reservoir. Like the Humpy this is not a particularly rugged fly but a moderate amount of damage does not hurt its effectiveness. You can keep it in top shape longer by coating its shellback with a thin layer of cement. Use saddle hackles on your larger Humpies, neck hackles on the smaller ones.

DOUBLE HUMPY

Hook: *Mustad 9671, 9672 or equivalent, sizes 6-10.*
Thread: *Yellow or red monocord, 3/0.*
Tail: *Deer body hair.*
Underbodies: *Yellow or red monocord.*
Wings and Shellbacks: *Formed of deer body hair with tips forming wings, upright and divided.*
Hackle: *Grizzly.*

This pattern came to eastern Idaho from Jackson Hole to find additional popularity. When I first saw the Double Humpy I thought that I had seen cats and dogs do that to each other, but not Humpies!

The story of how Joe Allen, a long-time Jackson Hole resident and fishing guide, conceived his Double Humpy in the winter of 1980-81 is well described by Paul Bruun in the May 1988 issue of *Fly Fisherman* magazine. Joe didn't get his inspiration from watching the greeting rites of dogs and cats. The story, humorous as it is, documents a typical inspiration for a new pattern, and the product of Joe's experience has proven to be superbly effective throughout the West. I wonder if Joe could multiply his success by creating a whole Humpy emergence on one hook.

In his article Paul also describes how Joe fishes his creation. One of the techniques is deadly whether used from a drift boat or when wading. It consists of dead drifting or twitching a fly as it floats toward cover, then pulling it underwater and stripping it in wet as it moves away from cover. Actually this technique has been used locally for years with the Bird's Stonefly during the giant and golden stonefly emergence, but Joe's Double Humpy is a much more versatile fly. It produces when presented in this manner not only when large stoneflies are emerging, but also when caddisflies or hoppers are the main fare available to trout. This means the Double Humpy is a consummate attractor: effective when fished dry or wet throughout the season. Joe deserves a load of credit for his creation.

DRY MUDDLER

Hook: *Mustad 9672, 79580 or equivalent, sizes 2-14.*
Thread: *Gray nylon, size 3/0 for smaller flies, size A for large ones.*
Tail: *Section of turkey quill.*
Body: *Gold sparkle tinsel, orange or yellow floss.*

Underwing: *Light brown kiptail overlain with white kiptail.*
Wings: *Pair of turkey quill segments mounted on either side of shank.*
Head: *Spun deer hair butts clipped to form head.*

"You're kidding!" Fred chuckled in reply to my comments as we drove one recent September down Highway 34 through quaking aspen and sagebrush country to fish the lower narrows above Blackfoot River Reservoir.

"The Muddler Minnow's a helluva streamer, but I've never tried it dry," he added.

"Give it a try," I replied.

At the end of the day the Dry Muddler had produced not only several nice trout, but a brace of 19-inch cutthroat and a 22- inch rainbow between us. Another convert was made to the dry version of Don Gapen's classic which is becoming an eastern Idaho favorite. My own experience with the Dry Muddler goes back to an unforgettable late August day in the early 1970s at the Railroad Ranch on Henry's Fork. There are good reasons for this pattern's rising popularity. It simulates larger stoneflies and thus is effective in season when dead drifted on faster waters. It simulates terrestrials such as hoppers, crickets and moths. When tied in appropriate colors it is effective dead drifted, twitched or skittered on the surface of all types of waters: from high gradient sections, to slow moving meadow stretches to still waters. It even simulates the giant orange sedge which in autumn emerges from moderate and slow moving waters across the region. A full hollow hair head and collar and turkey quill segment wings mounted on either side of the shank give this pattern excellent buoyancy and stability. The Dry Muddler is exceptionally durable and because it can be tied with materials of various colors, as indicated above, it's very versatile.

GRAY HACKLE PEACOCK

Hook: *Mustad 7957B or equivalent, sizes 8-18.*
Thread: *Black nylon, 6/0.*
Tail: *Scarlet hackle fibers.*
Body: *Peacock herl fibers twisted around tying thread, then wrapped.*
Hackle: *Grizzly: one for wet flies, two for dry.*

Hackle flies do not have wings but in other aspects are constructed to simulate mayfly duns. Their use in European waters, from the Balkans to the British Isles, has been well documented for centuries. Mary Orvis Marbury discusses this use in the first part of her classic *Favorite Flies and Their Histories.* This discourse, as well as the entire book, gives the reader insight into the widespread origins of fly fishing and its eventual expansion to other continents through colonialism. In these new environments native techniques and tackle variations were evolved, but certain practices and items remained in use. Among these were such flies as the "Gray Hackle" and "Brown Hackle." Marbury's writings also include incidents of their common nineteenth century use in Colorado. Among these flies were those constructed with peacock herl bodies—common in Europe where the fish attracting qualities of this material have been known for centuries. In eastern Idaho the Gray Hackle Peacock and Brown Hackle Peacock have been favorite attractor patterns, wet or dry, for most of the twentieth century. Ease in construction as well as effectiveness will make any pattern popular. Such is the case with the Gray Hackle Peacock. Thus most fly shops in the area offer it, and it is found on the roster of flies constructed in most of the fly tying courses offered in the area.

GRAY WULFF

Hook: *Mustad 7957B or equivalent, sizes 6-16.*
Thread: *Black or gray nylon, 6/0.*
Wings: *Brown elk body hair tied upright and divided.*
Tail: *Several brown elk body hairs.*
Body: *Muskrat, beaver or other gray dubbing.*
Hackle: *Two blue dun.*

Lee Wulff created the Gray Wulff in 1929, and thus it is one of the original Wulff patterns intended for simulating mayflies on eastern waters much as New York's swift Ausable River. With this fly and the White Wulff he popularized the use of hair to wing flies, although he was not the first to use hair for this purpose. In any case the use of upright and divided hair to form wings was an idea that caught on. The idea produced such durable and high floating patterns that others were created by Wulff and Dan Bailey for western waters as well as those in the East. Now Wulff patterns are fished worldwide.

Although original Gray Wulffs were usually tied in sizes 8 to 12, in eastern Idaho they are also popular in sizes 14 and 16. In small sizes they simulate a number of darker mayfly duns and are used mainly on faster waters of such streams as lower Henry's Fork, Falls River and the South Fork of the Snake. The larger Wulffs are used as dry attractor patterns on all faster streams but specifically are excellent for gray drakes on many area streams. Two other Wulff patterns, the Grizzly Wulff and the Badger Wulff, are popular in eastern Idaho as fast water attractor patterns. Like the Gray Wulff these patterns use elk body hair for the upright and divided wings as well as the tail. On both these patterns yellow dubbing is used to form the body. The Badger Wulff is finished with two badger hackles; the Grizzly Wulff is finished with two grizzly hackles.

HUMPY

Hook: *Mustad 7957B, 3906 or equivalent, sizes 6-18.*
Thread: *Monocord, 3/0, of colors discussed in text.*
Tail: *Dark brown stiff elk or moose stocking hair.*
Shellback: *Formed from bunch of elk or deer body hair with tips forming wings.*
Wings: *Upright and divided.*
Hackle: *Combinations discussed in text.*

As with the Woolly Worm, Renegade or Sofa Pillow no list of popular western flies would be complete without the Humpy. The saga of the Humpy's origin goes on and will probably remain a source of friendly discussion for years to come. The Humpy is known as such in Idaho and Wyoming; however in much of Montana it is known as the Goofus Bug, and this has added to the uncertainty of its origin. It has undergone a genesis in the past 20 years which has made it more durable. Much of the credit for this must go to Jack Dennis of Jackson, Wyoming who has substituted highly durable elk or moose stocking for the deer body hair of the tail. Also for large and medium sized Humpies, Jack has introduced more durable elk body hair in place of deer body hair for forming the shellback and wings. In addition, the original hackling of the Humpy (two grizzly hackles) has been expanded to combinations of grizzly, ginger, brown and badger. Likewise the use of appropriately colored tying thread results in yellow, green, cream, red or orange Humpies. Thus there is a wide array of Humpies based on hackle and thread color, and with use of dyed elk hair and deer hair the march of variations goes on. All are popular as high riding attractor patterns in eastern Idaho waters, large or small. In these waters fly size is the most important factor of choice. For example, Humpies in sizes 10 and 12 are standards when green drakes are on the surface of the Henry's Fork in the Chester to Ashton reach. Humpies from size six to eighteen are in popular use. And if all these variations and uses are not enough a new one, the Double Humpy created by Joe Allen of Jackson, Wyoming, is becoming popular in eastern Idaho.

IRRESISTIBLE

Hook: Mustad 7957B or equivalent, sizes 6-16.

Thread: Gray nylon; 6/0 for smaller flies, 3/0 for larger flies.

Tail: Dark brown elk or moose fibers.

Body: Spun deer hair clipped to shape.

Wings: White calf tail, upright and divided.

Hackle: One brown, one grizzly.

When first seeing an Irresistible one thinks: "This must be a western pattern." In every sense it is, but it originated in the East, and most sources credit it to Harry Darbee the renowned fly tier of Roscoe, New York in the Catskill Mountains. Its construction is similar to that of the older Rat-Faced McDougall, and with passage of time and the inevitable issue of variations the differences between the two have become less distinct. The original Irresistible appears to have been constructed with brown hackle and whitetail deer body hair wings and tail. The original Rat-Faced McDougall appears to have been constructed with ginger hackle, ginger hackle fiber tail and white calf tail wings. Both patterns have a spun deer hair body clipped in the shape of a half cone with flat ventral surface—the base at the front of the fly and the apex to the rear. An upright and divided white calf tail wing and massive spun, clipped deer hair body makes this fly highly visible. The clipped deer hair body also adds buoyancy, and when the fly is properly constructed it is very durable.

All of these assets have helped make the Irresistible a very popular fast water attractor in eastern Idaho. Another variation popular in eastern Idaho is the Adams Irresistible in which grizzly hackle tips are used for wings and dark elk or moose stocking hairs for the tail. Compared to the Renegade, Humpy and Royal Wulff the Irresistible is more difficult and time consuming to tie because it must be removed from the vise while shaping the body. Thus it is not used as much as these three attractor patterns.

NORTH FORK FLY

Hook: Mustad 7957B or equivalent, sizes 8-14.

Thread: Black monocord, 3/0.

Tail: Goose quill section dyed red or yellow.

Body: Full, formed of peacock herl spiralled around tying thread.

Wing: White kiptail tied Trude style, extending to hook bend.

Hackle: Two brown.

The North Fork Fly is Stan Yamamura's answer to demand for an effective dry attractor pattern that could be quickly and easily tied from abundant materials. His usual practice in determining the effectiveness of his creations was to fish them at the same time and in the same water with well known patterns of the same type. If his more easily tied creations were at least as effective as the well known pattern he would market them. Such was the case with the North Fork Fly which he created and marketed as an all purpose dry attractor pattern and as an alternative to the Royal Wulff, the Renegade or even the Humpy. Stan first tested this fly on the North Fork, as the Henry's Fork is known to many local anglers, and thus is the origin of its name. It is, however, an effective dry attractor pattern on riffles and runs in all area streams. In addition it is also used effectively as a wet attractor.

The North Fork Fly is quickly and easily tied by attaching the goose quill tail, then forming the tapered body from peacock herl wrapped around the tying thread to provide durability. Next, the downwing of white calf tail, with tips extending to the hook bend, is tied in; then the fly is finished with two or three turns of two dry fly quality brown hackles. The resulting fly rides well in broken waters and is very visible because of the white kiptail wing and yellow or red goose quill segment tail.

PROFESSOR

Hook: Mustad 7957B or equivalent, sizes 8-16.

Thread: Black nylon, 6/0.

Wings: Formed of speckled mallard flank or barred teal flank; upright and divided in dry versions,

downwing in wet version.

Tail: Scarlet hackle fibers.

Body: Yellow floss.

Rib: Flat silver mylar or tinsel.

Hackle: Brown neck: one for wet version, two for dry version.

This venerable pattern has been in use on the North American continent for nearly a century. According to Mary Orvis Marbury in her book *Favorite Flies and Their Histories* it was named for one of its proponents, Professor John Wilson who resided in Scotland in the early nineteenth century. The distinguishing mark of the Professor, of course, is its yellow silk body. In eastern Idaho this light colored fly has been used effectively for decades as a wet emerger for caddisflies and mayflies in streams at or near their base flows. It is also used with good results as a dry fly, probably because of the presence of lighter colored caddisfly and mayfly species and small, light colored stonefly species. Locally popular wet versions are tied with a downwing formed of speckled mallard flank fibers with natural tips extending to the hook bend and with sparse brown hackle. The dry version popularly used in this area has upright and divided wings formed of speckled mallard flank fibers, or barred teal flank and full brown hackle. One common dry variation used during late summer on many waters has a red tag. This is used to simulate the *Isoperla mormoni* species of stonefly known as the Mormon Girl. Some eastern Idaho fly fishers indicate that this version of the Professor is the forerunner of the many wet and dry patterns named "Mormon Girl."

RENEGADE

Hook: *Mustad 7957B, 3906 or equivalent, sizes 6-18.*
Thread: *Black nylon, 6/0.*
Tip: *Gold tinsel.*
Aft Hackle: *Two brown saddle or neck.*
Body: *Full, formed of peacock herls spiralled around tying thread.*
Fore Hackle: *Two white saddle or neck.*

Fore and aft patterns are those hackled at opposite ends of the shank. Fore and afts are represented by patterns from around the world, but their origin is probably in continental Europe where they have been popular for centuries. In this country they are identified mainly with western waters—the Renegade being the best known representative. Its use in Pacific Coast and Rocky Mountain states has been described in many documents. The Renegade appears to have been created in the 1930s by Taylor "Beartracks" Williams who at that time resided in the Sun Valley area of Idaho and fished its waters. The "Beartracks" preserve on Little Wood River, about 15 miles southwest of the village of Carey, was purchased by the State of Idaho from the Hemingway family and is named for Williams.

The directions given are for the traditional dry version. The wet version is constructed in the same manner except that wet fly quality white and brown hackles are used. The Renegade is made more durable by spiralling peacock herl fibers around the tying thread, then wrapping them to form the body. When tying Renegades in larger sizes underwrap the body with thin peacock green chenille to conserve peacock herl. Popular variations of the Renegade used in eastern Idaho include the Reverse Renegade (brown hackle fore, white hackle aft), Royal Renegade (red floss or Flashabou center section in body as in the Royal Wulff), and Henry's Lake Renegade (omit tip, single brown hackles fore and aft, red floss or Flashabou rib). All these variations retain the peacock herl body of the original. The Double Renegade is also a popular variation. It is tied on a 3X long hook (i.e. Mustad 9672), sizes 6-14 and consists of two peacock

herl body segments with fore, mid and aft hackles in such combinations as white-brown-brown, white-brown-grizzly and brown-white-brown. A red or gold tag is optional. The Double Renegade is used mainly as a wet attractor fly in still waters. Eastern Idaho anglers also use it during the giant and golden stonefly emergence, although it has largely been replaced by the Super Renegade.

ROYAL WULFF

Hook: *Mustad 7957B or equivalent, sizes 8-18.*
Thread: *Black nylon, 6/0.*
Wings: *White calf tail or body hair upright and divided.*
Tail: *Several dear body hairs.*
Body: *Peacock herl spiralled around tying thread divided in the middle by band of red floss.*
Hackle: *Two dark brown.*

Lee Wulff developed his dry flies by 1929. Later Dan Bailey named them the Wulff flies and with Lee added more patterns. The principle feature of the Wulff dry flies are upright and divided hair wings constructed of calf tail, bucktail, deer body hair or elk body hair and a tail of the same material except in the Royal Wulff which has a tail of deer hair. Many of the Wulff dry flies remain superbly effective attractor patterns and the Royal Wulff is perhaps the best known and most widely used of these. The American origins of the Royal Wulff go back to 1878 when John Hailey of New York City created the Royal Coachman. This fly in turn has its origin in the old English pattern, the Coachman. In any case, the Royal Wulff is a marriage of the Wulff series wing construction with the peacock herl body-red floss mid rib of the Royal Coachman. The Royal Coachman body construction has been adopted in other patterns such as the Royal Coachman Streamer, Royal Renegade, Royal Trude and Wright's Royal.

In eastern Idaho the Royal Wulff is used not only on fast waters but on all types including still waters such as high mountain lakes where it is a standard. Few dry patterns are in such widespread use in eastern Idaho as the Royal Wulff. It is as durable as it is effective, and it is one of the most beautiful patterns created. It can be argued that the Royal Trude, considered part of the Trude series of flies originally developed on Island Park waters in eastern Idaho, is a variation of the Royal Wulff.

BUCKTAIL CADDIS

Hook: *Mustad 9672 or equivalent, sizes 4-12.*
Thread: *Black monocord, 3/0.*
Body: *Orange floss.*
Rib: *Furnace saddle hackle.*

Wing: *Tied from mule deer rear flank hair.*
Head: *Trimmed butts of deer hair to form wing.*

The Bucktail Caddis or Caddis Bucktail, whichever way you call it, is a very effective fly. When Stan Yamamura operated "Stan's Flies" out of Idaho Falls in the 1960s and 1970s to supply retail outlets from southwestern Montana through eastern Idaho, the Bucktail Caddis was one of his best sellers. Its popularity has waned somewhat since the introduction of Al Troth's Elk Hair Caddis, a pattern which is constructed in a similar manner. But the "Caddis Buck," as it is often called in eastern Idaho, is still favored by many local fly fishers, particularly as a large adult stonefly imitation. This is truly a pattern of the Northwest, and through the years tiers throughout the region having created effective variations. Some variations are used as far east as Michigan to simulate the large mayfly, *Hexagenia limbata*. The most popular version used in eastern Idaho is tied without a tail and consists of an orange floss body palmered with a reddish brown saddle or neck hackle. Hair from the rear flanks of mule deer have a natural curve, and it is used to give the wing of locally favorite versions a concave shape. The tips of the wing extend just beyond the hook bend, and the butts of this bunch of hair, when clipped close to the finishing knot, form the head. The result is a buoyant and visible fly which is not only ideal for imitating larger caddisflies and stoneflies in faster waters but is durable and easy to tie.

ELK HAIR CADDIS

Hook: *Mustad 7957B or equivalent, sizes 8-18.*
Thread: *Nylon, 6/0, color to match natural insect.*
Body: *Dubbing or tying thread of col-*

or to match natural insect.
Hackle: *Brown or ginger palmered around body.*
Wing: *Cream elk rump hair.*

Al Troth's Elk Hair Caddis is more than an effective dry fly. It is a classic in dry fly symmetry and in simplicity. As with all exceptionally durable and effective patterns it has caught on around the world.

With respect to numbers, caddisflies are the dominant aquatic insect available to trout in eastern Idaho waters, and at any given time during the season some of their species are emerging on these waters. Thus they are available to trout throughout the season. Because of this availability and the above mentioned properties, the Elk Hair Caddis is a very popular pattern here. Many local fly fishers use this pattern with a gold, olive or tan dubbed body. But a variation that is also popular is the use of a thread body which can be wrapped more quickly than dubbing. It is also less massive and porous than a dubbed body, thus it has better floating properties.

The Elk Hair Caddis is used to simulate small stoneflies, hoppers or moths as well as its ever present and abundant namesake. Thus it is used on essentially all waters throughout the season in eastern Idaho. This results in its use in sizes ranging from eight to eighteen. A days supply of Elk Hair Caddis, particularly in the thread body version, can be tied up very quickly. Tie in the hackle at the bend. Wrap the thread body then the hackle. Tie in the wing with the tips extending to the bend and whip finish. Take it from the vise and clip the butts of the wing to form the head.

GODDARD CADDIS

Hook: *Mustad 7957B, 94840 or equivalent, sizes 8-18.*
Thread: *Gray nylon, 3/0.*
Body: *Deer, antelope or caribou hair spun on rear two-thirds of shank,*

then clipped to shape.
Antennae: *Two stripped hackle stems or pieces of monofilament.*
Hackle: *One ginger or brown.*

The Goddard Caddis, truly an international pattern, was created by John Goddard who intended it to simulate caddisflies in still waters. It proved effective when used in the wave breakline along shores of lakes and reservoirs in the British Isles because of its buoyancy, profile and visibility. Soon, contemplative fly fishers in different places recognized that this fly was also ideal for fishing during caddis emergences in moving water. Thus, around the world the Goddard Caddis is now a standard fast-water pattern.

In eastern Idaho there are reaches on nearly every stream where the Goddard Caddis is effective in riffles, runs and other fast water. Although the densest caddis emergences occur in the early season, certain species emerge from area streams well into autumn. Thus fishing caddis patterns, adult or pupa, is always a choice to consider.

When the art of spinning hollow hair is mastered the Goddard Caddis is easily tied. It is best to spin the hollow hair onto the rear two-thirds of the shank, whip finish the tying thread, remove the hook from the vise and then trim the body to shape. Next return the hook to the vise, tie in the antennae and tie in a single hackle to finish the fly. The result is a durable, effective and high floating fly. Originally natural deer or antelope hair was used to form the body of the Goddard Caddis. A popular variation fished in eastern Idaho uses dyed amber deer hair to form the body.

Henryville Special

Hook: *Mustad 7957B, 94840 or equivalent, sizes 12-20.*
Thread: *Nylon, 6/0, same color as body.*
Body: *Tan, yellow or gray dubbing with palmered ginger hackle.*
Underwing: *Ginger hackle fiber tips extending to hook bend.*
Wings: *Overlapping duck quill slips flat over back.*
Hackle: *A few turns of ginger.*

This pattern was created by Hiram Brobst for use on Pennsylvania's Broadheads River. It is named after the reach on which it was originally effective. Now the Henryville Special is a standard adult caddis pattern in use in eastern Idaho (and throughout the world) where it is typically effective on medium gradient streams. A good example of such waters are the riffles and moderate gradient stretches of Henry's Fork in the Ashton-St. Anthony area where the early season caddis emergence is a boon to winterbound east Idaho fly fishers. Normally caddis species begin to emerge here in good numbers by mid April, and the Henryville Special in sizes 14 and 16 is very effective at this time. As on other such waters in the area it remains effective throughout the season because various caddis species emerge through autumn.

When viewed from the sides or top the predominant color of the Henryville Special is gray, like the natural insect, because of the duck quill wings. However, there are many body colors that can be used to make this fly simulate the coloring of the caddisfly emerging at a given time. These include amber, olive or tan. First tie in a light ginger hackle at the bend of the hook, then dubbing to match the color of the natural insect. Wrap the dubbing forward, palmer the hackle over it, then clip the fibers from the tip of the hackle. Tie in the underwing then the overlapping duck quill segments to form the wings. At the point where the wings are tied in wrap a few turns of ginger hackle, then whip finish the head.

Midge

Hook: *Mustad 94840 or equivalent, sizes 16-22.*
Thread: *Nylon, 6/0, color to match natural insect.*
Tail: *Optional; sparse hackle fibers.*
Body: *Tying thread or sparse dubbing, color to match natural insect.*
Wings: *Optional; upright and divided, postwing or downwing of kiptail.*
Hackle: *A few turns of black, brown, ginger or grizzly.*

December through March is the "off season" for fishing in eastern Idaho. Many waters, mainly portions of the trunk streams, remain open to fishing during these months, but good conditions for dry fly fishing only happen occasionally. East Idaho winters are not all fluster and freeze, however, as bluebird days of sunshine, balmy temperatures and still air occur. During these days a phenomena takes place that results in some good dry fly fishing. This is the midge emergence. Chironomids, or midges, emerge year-round, but in other seasons their availability to trout is accompanied by that of other insects on which trout usually key. Locally the winter midge emergence is called the "snowfly hatch," and it peaks during the midday hours on the bluebird or mild days of winter. On many of these days "snowflies" are alone on the surfaces of riffle areas of local streams. Although pupa imitations fished in the surface film bring more action, dry fly fishing at this time is also effective.

In general dry midges are sparsely tied on hooks of size 16 or less. Frequently tying thread is used to form the body. Optional wings, tied down, clumped or upright and divided are of light colored material for visibility. Optional tails are sparse, and the fly is finished with only a few turns of hackle. The materials mentioned above can be varied with respect to color resulting in a wide variety of patterns all of which must be presented on light tippets.

Spent Partridge Caddis

Hook: *Mustad 7957B or equivalent, sizes 12-20.*
Thread: *Nylon, 6/0 prewaxed, color to match body.*
Body: *Amber, gray, olive or tan dubbing.*
Wings: *Two brown mottled partridge hackles on top and overlapping.*
Thorax: *Peacock herl.*
Hackle: *One brown and one grizzly tied in over thorax and clipped flat on bottom.*

In the minds of most fly fishers, Mike and Sheralee Lawson, are associated with the Henry's Fork in the Island Park area of eastern Idaho because of their business, the Henry's Fork Anglers at Last Chance. For years Mike has created fly patterns for that area which are also effective on many other waters. The Spent Partridge Caddis, which dates back to the 1970s, is one of these, and by any measure is one of his most successful.

Mike originally created his pattern to simulate the smaller caddisflies that are found at many locations on Henry's Fork. The hackles are clipped from the bottom of the fly to add stability, and partridge, sage hen or grouse are used for the wing rather than hen hackle because of their color and ability to retain the proper shape when wet. Many fly tiers in eastern Idaho construct this pattern with tan, gray or amber bodies in addition to Mike's original olive body. With any of these colors the pattern is highly effective. In fact the pattern is now tied and used to simulate caddis of all sizes. In particular the Spent Partridge Caddis seems most effective when used to simulate egg laying female caddis. These occur throughout the season because caddis flies are found in nearly every eastern Idaho stream. Specific examples of when caddis activity dominates are during the early season on the lower Henry's Fork and during the late season on the South Fork of the Snake River and on the Big Lost River. At these times the Spent Partridge Caddis will perform spectacularly.

THE MEAT GETTER

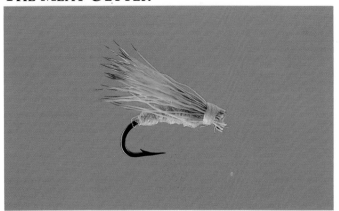

Hook: *Mustad 94838 or equivalent, sizes 14-16.*
Thread: *Yellow or tan nylon, 6/0.*
Body: *Yellow or tan poly yarn.*

Wing: *Stiff elk or deer body hair. Set wing at about 45 degree angle with thread wraps just behind base.*

I first met Bob Bean and some of his fishing pals only recently at their watering hole in Blackfoot's B & B Bait Shop. As the good natured ribbing and half serious small talk progressed I realized that this self-effacing, recently retired elementary school teacher was a local institution. I regret that I did not meet him earlier.

"Fly tying specialty?" he replied with a grin to my question. "Heck, I just keep tying until I find something that catches fish, then I just stick with it. Kind of like finding a fishing spot that suits your fancy, so you keep on coming back!"

One of the flies that he has created that must suit his fancy is the caddis imitation he calls The Meat Getter. When I picked one up a narrative on its use and name began.

"We've all used it for years on the spring creeks above American Falls Reservoir and other places, especially early in the season, and you know it sure brings 'em up when caddis are on the water. But its just as good when mayflies are emerging. See how the wings are tied in? Just dress it well, drift it on a long leader and hang on for the action as something always takes it".

The Meat Getter resembles any downwing caddis imitation except it is tied without a hackle making it ride low in the water. Its poly yarn body is about as thick as the dubbed body on a traditional Elk Hair Caddis. But a specific difference is the higher angle at which its wing is set by using thread wraps in a way similar to that of wedging hair or hackle tip wings in place on mayfly dun patterns. The result gives not only the impression of caddis wings but that of the unfurling wings of a mayfly emerger.

MAYFLIES

ADAMS

Hook: *Mustad 7857B or equivalent, sizes 8-20.*
Thread: *Black nylon, 6/0.*
Wings: *Grizzly hackle tips, upright and divided.*

Tail: *Light elk rump hair or dark moose or elk hock hair.*
Body: *Dubbed muskrat, beaver or light gray artificial dubbing.*
Hackle: *One brown, one grizzly.*

Originated by Leonard Halliday in Michigan in the early 1920s, the Adams is one of the most popular flies ever created. It was originally used on Michigan's Boardman River, and its effectiveness was described by Charles Adams, an Ohio native. Thus Halliday named his fly after Adams. Since those days the Adams has become internationally renowned.

In eastern Idaho the Adams is used to simulate several mayfly species and even caddisfly species. Specifically, the Adams in sizes 14 and 16 is effectively used to simulate *Callibaetis* species, the most common mayflies found on area lakes and ponds. *Callibaetis*, commonly known as speckled duns, emerge from May to October in still and slow moving streams, so it is good practice to carry Adams whenever fishing these water types. Also, Adams in sizes 16-18 are effective imitations of the *Paraleptophlebia* species of mayflies. These mayflies, commonly called mahogany duns, emerge from area freestone streams of moderate flow rates from August to October. Duns and emergers are a favorite food form of trout. These specific uses

will surely bear fruit, but so will variations of this storied fly. A popular variation is the Female Adams which is tied with a yellow or orange egg sac to simulate female duns depositing eggs. Other variations in popular use in eastern Idaho include the Yellow Adams and Cream Adams which simulate *Stenonema* and *Epeorus* species respectively, and the Peacock Adams, which is used as a fast water attractor pattern.

BLUE WINGED OLIVE

Hook: *Mustad 7957B or equivalent, sizes 16-20.*
Thread: *Black nylon, 6/0.*
Wings: *Loop wing formed of four gadwall fibers, each wing.*
Tail: *Ends of monofilament fibers, 0.006 diam. used to form beam.*

Beam: *Two blue monofilament fibers tied to hook shank and extending to rear to form body.*
Body: *Extended body formed of dark olive Antron yarn.*
Hackle: *Two blue dun neck.*

The most widespread mayflies found in eastern Idaho waters are *Baetis* species, commonly known as blue winged olives. Not only are they found in most moving water types at all altitudes, but they emerge in nearly all seasons. Riffles and shallow runs host them in the best numbers, and fish feed on emerged duns drifting on the surface. Blue winged olives drift for longer times in cooler weather, such as in early spring and in late autumn, making them easily available. Thus trout and whitefish key on them meaning that drifting duns provide major fly fishing opportunities. Important early season blue winged olive emergences occur on lower Henry's Fork, Warm River and on spring creeks above American Falls Reservoir. Important autumn emergences occur on lower Henry's Fork, on the South Fork of the Snake River and on middle portions of Big Lost River. The tiny blue winged olives, a genus other than *Baetis*, accompanies the Blue Winged Olive emergence from the lower Henry's Fork and South Fork of the Snake River during mid and late September.

When presenting dun imitations one must achieve a drag free drift through the feeding lane of a rising fish. Delicate tippets, light rods and lines and an approach quartering from above to present the fly before the leader, are the rules. Use blue winged olive imitations in sizes 16 and smaller.

Several imitations of blue winged olive duns are popular in eastern Idaho. An Adams or a Cahill tied with a dubbed olive body and with upright and divided wings of blue dun hackle fibers are both effective. Bing Lempke's Extended Body Blue Winged Olive, pictured and described above, is the most notable of the native patterns. Sizes 18 and 20 are most useful. In structure Bing's Pale Morning Dun is similar to this pattern. It is tied with a tail of three monofilament fibers, body of light olive dubbing, wings or mallard primary fibers and ginger hackle.

CARMICHAEL

Hook: *Mustad 7959B or equivalent, sizes 8-18.*
Thread: *Brown nylon, 6/0.*
Wings: *Grizzly hackle tips.*
Tail: *Dark brown elk or moose hair.*

Body: *Pink dubbing; Carmichael Indispensable has yellow floss tip and pink dubbing body.*
Hackle: *Brown and grizzly.*

Bob Carmichael is a Jackson Hole legend. For decades, starting in the 1930s, he and his postmistress wife, Fran, ran a tackle shop at the post office in Moose, Wyoming. Gruff, honest and knowledgeable Bob dispensed merchandise and information to those fishing the scenic Jackson Hole and Yellowstone country. His flies where prized by all for their quality and effectiveness. He had flies appropriate for all conditions and instructions for their use. One of his creations, the Carmichael, a Jackson Hole standard, crossed the Teton Range into Idaho to become popular on the waters of Teton Basin and on the South Fork of the Snake River drainage. It was also used farther south on streams such as Stump and Crow creeks which drain east from Idaho into Wyoming's Salt River. On all these waters the Carmichael is preferred over the Adams, which it resembles, by many anglers. The main difference between the two flies, both of which are fished on various water types, is that the Carmichael has a body of dubbed pink fur while the Adams has variations with tails of mixed brown and grizzly fibers, light elk, dark elk or moose hair or even golden pheasant tippet fibers. There is another Carmichael; the Carmichael Indispensable, in which a yellow floss tip and pink fur dubbing form the body. Many fly fishers prefer this variation over both the Adams and Carmichael, but all three are tremendously effective, particularly in waters from which many mayfly species emerge.

GRAY FOX VARIANT

Hook: *Mustad 94840 or equivalent, sizes 14-18.*
Thread: *Yellow nylon, 6/0.*
Tail: *Ginger hackle fibers.*

Body: *Stripped light brown saddle hackle stem close wrapped.*
Hackle: *Two ginger neck slightly oversized.*

Famous names from the past are associated with this fly. Its origins are found in the streams of New York's Catskill Mountains and in personalities such as Preston Jennings and Art Flick. Most of the credit for developing the Gray Fox Variant must go to Jennings whose landmark work *A Book of Trout Flies*, published in 1935 is a classic which presents the Catskill style of tying mayfly dun imitations as well as other styles including that of variants such as the Gray Fox Variant. Variants are tied without wings and with oversized hackle to give the fly the ability to land lightly on the water when presented to wary fish.

As with other effective flies originating in the eastern United States, the Gray Fox Variant migrated west. In eastern Idaho this fly is used to imitate small mayfly duns and is presented with delicate leaders on still waters or on shallow riffles holding wary feeding fish. In these uses it is rarely presented in sizes greater than 14.

The Gray Fox Variant is easy to tie, however particular attention must be paid when constructing the body. A saddle hackle is used for this purpose. The stem is stripped of all fibers, then it is immersed in water for a few hours before use. Absorbed water gives the stem flexibility to be wrapped around the hook shank without splitting, and it then should be wrapped starting with the thinner end. After the fly is finished the wrapped stem forming the body should be allowed to dry for several hours then finished with a few coats of head cement. The result is a fly of considerable beauty and durability.

GREEN DRAKE

Hook: *Mustad 7957B or equivalent, size 12.*
Thread: *Black nylon, 2/0.*
Wings: *Goose primary sections with rounded tips.*
Tail: *Extension of three black monofilament fibers, 0.006" diameter, secured along hook shank to form beam.*

Underbody: *Art Foam strip, 3/8" wide, wrapped along shank and up beam.*
Egg Sac: *Two peacock herl fibers.*
Rib: *Size A yellow nylon.*
Body: *Peacock olive floss.*
Hackle: *One each grizzly neck hackle dyed yellow and blue dun.*

The most celebrated mayfly emergence from eastern Idaho waters is that of the green drake in the Harriman State Park reach of the Henry's Fork. This emergence, one of the most concentrated of green drakes known, begins in mid June, lasts until mid July and draws fly fishers from around the globe. In eastern Idaho it is rivalled in attention only by the giant and golden stonefly emergences on the Henry's Fork and the South Fork of the Snake River. The most suitable habitat for green drakes is slower moving waters with silty bottoms having vegetation with exposed roots and stems. There is an abundance of this habitant in the Harriman State Park reach of the Henry's Fork, but good green drake habitat is found in other eastern Idaho streams. There is an excellent emergence on the lower Henry's Fork between Chester and Ashton dams. There are locally important emergences on the upper Blackfoot River, Robinson Creek and the South Fork tributaries including Bear Creek and McCoy Creek. Even as unlikely a stream as the South Fork of the Snake River, from which most silt is scoured, has a fishable green drake emergence.

Green drake duns are suitably simulated by large Humpies, Grizzly Wulffs or Gray Wulffs. However a number of specific green drake patterns that have evolved locally have gained popularity. Bing Lempke's Extended Body Green Drake is pictured above. Bing developed this pattern in the late 1970s with the pattern shown being the culmination of his efforts. Now his Green Drake is recognized throughout the fly fishing world as an effective pattern and a work of art.

All green drake dun patterns are best presented on a dead drift from aside and above. During the peak of the daily emergence many fish will be taking duns which begin emerging when water temperatures reach the mid-50s Fahrenheit. Thus it becomes possible to present flies to very large fish and the chances are good that an exhilarating encounter will result.

HAIR WING DUN

Hook: *Mustad 94840 or equivalent, sizes 12-20.*
Thread: *Gray nylon, 6/0.*
Tail: *Brown hackle fibers tied in the shape of a "V" with three or four fibers per side.*

Body: *Gray dubbing.*
Hackle: *One brown and one grizzly mounted at mid shank.*
Wing: *Tied downwing as in elk hair caddis from calf elk hair, gray at base and blond at tips.*

The Hair Wing Dun, a new concept of tying mayfly duns, is another contribution to fly tying by Rene Harrop. His account of the inspiration for the Hair Wing Dun is provided in the June 1988 issue of *Fly Fisherman* magazine. Also revealed is the versatility and effectiveness which makes this concept so important.

Rene, mostly associated in fly fishing with the Henry's Fork in the Island Park area, is from the Ririe area of eastern Idaho and had many of his early fly fishing experiences on the South Fork of the Snake River. Over the years creation of fly tying concepts, art and fly fishing techniques have made Rene, Bonnie and their children, Idaho's first family with respect to fly fishing.

The Catskill tradition of tying mayfly duns has been familiar to the fly tying world for decades. Rene's concept is a noticeable departure from this technique. It uses a downwing constructed of calf elk hair for visibility and construction properties, a split tail of hackle fibers to add stability and hackles mounted at the mid-point of the shank then clipped at the bottom to give physical stability and artistic balance. Any mayfly dun can be simulated by the Hair Wing Dun simply by changing the hook size and the colors of construction materials. The instructions given above use materials to tie an Adams by the Hair Wing Dun concept. Rene first tested the Hair Wing Dun concept on the waters of the lower Henry's Fork near his home in St. Anthony. Here he observed that this pattern had the buoyancy and visibility to be easily fished in fast, broken waters and was also well suited for fishing in slower waters because of its profile and delicate structure. Now patterns tied with this concept are being fished throughout the world.

LIGHT CAHILL

Hook: *Mustad 7957B or equivalent, sizes 8-18.*
Thread: *Light yellow nylon, 6/0.*
Wings: *Mallard flank fibers dyed*

wood duck, upright and divided.
Tail: *Several light elk hairs.*
Body: *Light cream dubbing.*
Hackle: *Two ginger.*

The Light Cahill is one of the best known representatives of the Catskill mayfly dun tying technique. The technique originated with fly tiers fishing streams draining these southeastern New York mountains and is characterized by flies having a slender tapered body, upright and divided wings formed of delicate materials such as wood duck flank fibers, turns of stiff, light colored hackles and a sparse tail. Most sources credit Daniel Cahill as the originator of this fly.

In eastern Idaho the Light Cahill is used throughout the fishing season to simulate all species of light colored mayflies. Sizes 10 to 18 are most popular. Light colored mayflies emerge from all water types thus the Light Cahill is used on many waters. Specifically it is used on area waters to simulate *Stenonema* mayflies, commonly represented by the *terminatum* species. These inhabit many area drainages and emerge from August to October. The most extensive population of these mayflies exists in the South Fork of the Snake River. Thus the Light Cahill is perhaps the most commonly used mayfly dun imitation on that stream. Popular variations of the Light Cahill used in this area are the Quill Cahill in which a stripped peacock herl is used to form the body and the Dark Cahill in which dubbed muskrat fur is used to form the body. Originally, wings of the Light Cahill were formed of lemon wood duck flank fibers. This material is becoming difficult to obtain, thus speckled mallard flank dyed lemon yellow is commonly substituted to construct the wings.

LIGHT VARIANT

Hook: *Mustad 94840 or equivalent, sizes 8-18.*
Thread: *Cream nylon, 6/0.*
Wings: *Ginger hackle tips upright and divided.*
Tail: *Several light elk hairs.*
Body: *Light cream dubbing.*
Hackle: *One cream and one ginger, or two ginger, one size oversized.*

The Light Variant is another pattern that has crossed the mountains from Jackson Hole to find popularity in Idaho. Of those that have done so this one is perhaps the most popular.

For years (starting in the 1940s) Roy Donnelly, a Pacific coast longshoreman, tied flies for Bob Carmichael's shop in Moose, Wyoming. His flies were praised by those who fished the swift, strong waters of Jackson Hole-Yellowstone country. Perhaps the most popular of these high floaters was the Light Variant which by the 1950s and 1960s was a standard, not only east of the Teton Range, but west of it in such waters as those in Teton Basin, the South Fork of the Snake River drainage and the Henry's Fork drainage. Traditionally variants tied for European and eastern North American waters were constructed with oversized hackles and without wings. Roy Donnelly, however, tied his Light Variant with hackle tip wings, and along with the Adams and Carmichael it was among the first popular flies in this part of the West tied with wings constructed of this material.

In eastern Idaho many fly fishers still prefer to use the Light Variant over the Light Cahill when fishing faster waters. But with the advent of the Blond Humpy and Gray Fox Variant its popularity has waned somewhat. It is an easy fly to tie with the principle point of attention being that stiff, oversized hackle must be used to prepare proper dressings. The hackle tip wings, tied upright and divided, are sized properly for the hook used and thus are not as long as the hackle.

PALE MORNING DUN

Hook: *Mustad 94840 or equivalent, sizes 16-20.*
Thread: *Light olive nylon, 6/0.*
Tail: *Three light cream moose leg hairs.*
Body: *Blend of olive, yellow and white dubbing.*
Wings: *White calf body hair.*
Hackle: *One sandy dun tied parachute style around wing.*

With the exception of blue winged olives (*Baetis* sp.), pale morning duns (several *Ephemerella sp.*) are the most widespread mayflies found in eastern Idaho streams. The duns and emergers are available to trout on stream surfaces from as early as mid May to late September. In the early season when water temperature plays a major role their emergence is dependent on weather and runoff conditions. For example, on the lower Henry's Fork they appear in late May, while on the runoff and irrigation water laden South Fork of the Snake River they usually don't appear until mid or late July. In the Willow Creek drainage the pale morning duns emerge in early June and from the Teton and Blackfoot rivers from mid June to early July depending on runoff conditions.

Because of this widespread occurrence many versions of the pale morning dun have been used. For general use Bing Lempke's extended body pattern is as effective as any, but other hackled patterns such as the Light Cahill or Light Variant can be used on faster waters. On smoother waters no-hackle and parachute patterns are best because of their smaller surface impression. The pattern described and pictured above is Paul Bowen's Parachute Pale Morning Dun which is ideal for smooth waters. The white hair post wing makes it highly visible, and the parachute style hackle gives it stability. These features also make Paul's pattern suitable for use on faster waters such as on the South Fork of the Snake River where it has proven effective during pale morning dun surface activity.

As with all small mayfly patterns Pale Morning Duns should be presented to rising fish fly first from above, dead drifted and as drag free as possible. This is increasingly important the smoother the water and requires lightweight tackle and fine, pliant leaders.

RAG WING DUN

Hook: *Mustad 94840 or equivalent, sizes 12-18.*
Thread: *Nylon, 6/0, color to match natural insect.*
Tail: *Speckled mallard flank fibers.*
Wing: *Sparkle Yarn clump canted at a 45-degree angle to the rear.*
Body: *Fly Rite dubbing of color to match natural insect.*
Thorax: *Slightly thicker than body and tied from the same material.*
Hackle: *Two hackles of color to match that of natural insect.*

Because of the emergence of various mayfly species in our area accomplished fly tiers tend to create an all purpose mayfly dun which will combine durability, effectiveness, simplicity and versatility into one. The Rag Wing Dun series is Wes Newman's answer to an all purpose pattern. He created it only a few years ago but after the past few seasons of use and fanfare it is becoming well known. Wes originally came from Twin Falls and has now lived in Idaho Falls for over 20 years. In this time he has established a reputation not only as one of Idaho's premier tiers of steelhead flies, but also as an innovative creator of locally effective patterns for trout. He is also an experienced fly fisher of local waters with a particular depth of knowledge on fishing the trunk streams.

Wes originally tied Rag Wing Duns with a dubbed rabbit fur body and thorax but changed to the synthetic Fly Rite because of its superior floating qualities. Sparkle Yarn wings and fibers from speckled mallard flank feathers, which Wes found to be effective on his patterns for small stoneflies, were also adopted for the tail. Hackles of various colors are used to approximate that of the subject dun. In order to ensure that the hackle stands upright Wes wraps them behind the wing over the dubbed thorax.

Some color schemes Wes uses are gray dubbing and grizzly hackle for speckled duns and mahogany duns, olive dubbing and mixed grizzly-brown hackle for blue winged olives and slate winged olives and cream dubbing and blue dun hackle for pale morning duns and slate cream duns. Rag Wing Dun sizes should be appropriate for the duns being imitated and are presented in the traditional dead drift manner, downstream to rising fish.

SPECKLED BIOT SPINNER

Hook: *Tiemco 100 or equivalent, size 16.*
Thread: *Cream nylon, 6/0.*
Tail: *Four or five stiff grizzly cock hackle fibers.*

Abdomen: *Light tan goose biot.*
Thorax: *Light tan dubbing.*
Wings: *Pair of gray Hungarian Partridge hackles tied spent.*

Bonnie Harrop created her Speckled Biot Spinner in 1987. She proved its effectiveness on the Henry's Fork, and now it is one of the Harrop's most sought after patterns. Bonnie has tied flies for about 20 years, and along with her husband Rene, has experienced the phenomenon that comes to all who produce perfection: demand. This demand is not only for patterns that are effective on the stream but also as art objects. Thus Bonnie and Rene have passed their tying skills on to their children Leslie Harrop Wheeler and Shayne Harrop. Now a tradition of creating superb patterns for specific life forms is emerging in this family from St. Anthony.

The spinner is the last stage of life for the adult mayfly, and except for egg laying flights perhaps the least fished by most anglers. After egg laying flights females of many species collapse onto the waters and their wings flatten to the surface as life ebbs away. These are spent spinners and a low, translucent profile makes them difficult to see. Spent spinners lying on the surface move only with the flow of water or by direction of the wind, thus they are easy for trout to eat. This means rewards for the angler encountering trout feeding on a spinner fall. For success in this encounter, which usually occurs early or late in the day, one must use delicate equipment to present a drag free float preferably from above and aside. Concentration is vital; one must be totally aware of the imitation drifting toward the feeding fish. Awareness, of course, is enhanced by nearness. Thus it is those with advanced wading or stalking skills who will most realize the rewards of fishing spent spinners.

————— STONEFLIES —————

BIRD'S STONEFLY

Hook: *Mustad 9672, 79580 or equivalent, sizes 2-12.*
Thread: *Orange monocord, 3/0.*
Tail: *Two pieces two-pound test monofilament.*
Body: *Orange floss or poly yarn.*

Rib: *Trimmed brown saddle hackle.*
Wing: *Elk mane tied downwing.*
Hackle: *Mixed furnace and brown saddles.*
Antennae: *Two pieces two-pound test monofilament.*

If there is a universally known adult stonefly pattern, then this is it. Dr. Calvert Bird of San Francisco created this superbly effective pattern, and like the Sofa Pillow it is meant to simulate adult stoneflies. Cal created stonefly nymph patterns which are also very effective. With respect to general use this pattern is probably the most popular of all stonefly patterns, however many tiers prefer the Sofa Pillow for reasons of simplicity.

With respect to appearance there are major differences between these two patterns. Whereas the Sofa Pillow rides high in the water because of its full squirrel tail wing and dense hackle, the Bird's Stonefly rides low in the water because of its flattened wing and clipped hackles on top and bottom surfaces. This makes the Bird's Stonefly less visible in low light conditions

and when one fishes the fly while facing the sun. This condition can be diminished significantly by tying in a bunch of white bucktail or calftail on top of the wing. The added visibility increases its effectiveness. This variation is gaining in popularity in eastern Idaho where Bird's Stonefly is a standard pattern used by bank and float anglers during stonefly emergences. Another use of this pattern that is gaining popularity is as a wet fly drifted by float anglers under bushes, overhangs, sweepers and other cover during the stonefly emergence.

LC MOOSE

Hook: *Mustad 9672 or equivalent, sizes 4-10.*
Thread: *Orange waxed flat nylon.*
Body: *Bleached or black elk hair overwrapped with tying thread covering rear 2/3 of shank.*
Tail: *Natural tips of bleached elk hair bunch used to form body.*

Rib: *Dark brown saddle hackle.*
Hackle: *Dark brown or gray dun saddle.*
Underwing: *Moose mane to form 1/3 of wing bulk.*
Overwing: *Bleached or dyed gray elk hair to form 2/3 of wing bulk.*
Collar: *Dark brown saddle hackle.*

Effective and durable patterns originate from fly fishing experience and fly tying talent. This unique pattern was created locally by two individuals with this experience and talent. Steve Christensen and Wendell Lewis are not only dentistry partners in Rexburg but on occasion fish together and tie flies together. Their LC Moose (L for Lewis and C for Christensen) is becoming well known for imitating adult giant and golden stoneflies on Rocky Mountain streams from Montana to Colorado.

Elk hair has always been one of the best natural materials for combining durability with buoyancy. Moose mane has the same properties, and thus Wendell suggests its use for a contrasting underwing. Steve suggests the use of black elk hair for forming the underbody and tail to represent egg-laying female stoneflies. Experience has further developed this pattern. An LC Moose tied with dark brown hackle and bleached elk hair wing is most effective during overcast skies, while an LC Moose tied with gray dun hackle and dyed gray elk hair is most effective during clear skies. Later versions have two pairs of rubber hackle legs mounted on top of the shank in front of the wings and the collar hackle wound through them. Experience has revealed to Steve and Wendell that black rubber hackle is most effective for use on larger flies. Orange rubber hackle is most effective on smaller flies which also make good hopper patterns. All versions of the LC Moose are effective when dead drifted, twitched or skittered over the surface during adult stonefly activities or during the hopper season.

MARCELLA'S TROUT FLY

Hook: *Mustad 9672 or equivalent, sizes 4-6.*
Thread: *Black nylon, 2/0.*
Tail: *Straw colored elk rump hair.*
Rib: *Brown saddle hackle.*
Body: *Fluorescent orange yarn.*
Wing: *Brown from whitetail deer tail.*
Hackle: *Two furnace saddles.*

In 1935 Harvey and Marcella Oswald opened their store and gas station on First Street in Idaho Falls. In 1944 they moved to a new location on First Street. Their emphasis was now on selling sporting goods, and when fly suppliers would not reveal the skills of tying to Marcella she taught herself. In those days good pheasant hunting could be enjoyed just east of their store.

Through the years the area was developed into commercial, residential and professional property, during which time the Oswalds became one of eastern Idaho's foremost known outdoor couples. With their children they were active in hunting, trap shooting, dog training and fly fishing. Marcella sold her flies in the store or by custom order and her creations gained a reputation for durability and effectiveness on local waters. In addition she taught fly tying for many years through the Idaho Falls City Recreation Department. Hundreds of local tiers credit her with introducing them to this art.

There is not a food form that Marcella couldn't create a pattern for and which did not become locally popular. But the best known pattern that this celebrated lady created was Marcella's Trout Fly. She created this highly buoyant and fully dressed pattern in the early 1950s in response to demands for an effective and visible pattern for imitating the giant stoneflies that emerge profusely from the Henry's and South Forks of the Snake River and from the Teton River. Over the years she modified the

pattern. Her annual output of this fly alone measured in the hundreds of dozens.

She closed the store after Harvey's death in 1981 but continued to tie flies to fill custom orders. From 1982 to 1985 she worked at Ralph Alexander's Hackle Den, located where pheasants formerly abounded east of their store. She tied flies for the Hackle Den and her trout fly remained in demand. Now the Hackle Den is closed and Marcella mainly ties her Trout Fly for custom orders. One must look outside of the locally conceived stonefly patterns to such as Bing Lempke's Hopper, Mike Lawson's Spent Partridge Caddis or Rene Harrop's Hairwing Dun to find another locally conceived pattern that rivals Marcella's Trout Fly in popularity.

MORMON GIRL

Hook: *Mustad 7957B or equivalent, sizes 10-16.*
Thread: *Black nylon, 6/0.*
Wings: *Upright and divided or downwing of mallard flank fibers.*
Egg Sac: *Red dubbing or floss.*
Rib: *Silver tinsel.*
Body: *Yellow dubbing, fur or floss.*
Hackle: *One or two brown.*

"Some of the old timers will tell you that this is supposed to be fully dressed just like its namesake when appearing in public!," Ralph Moon puckishly said as he gave me the dry version of the Mormon Girl pictured above. "I remember my dad using it here in Idaho back in the 1930s, so its origin could go as far back as 1910 or 1920," he added.

This is a fly of legend throughout the West and its origin comes from somewhere in Utah as can be deduced from its name. Into the early twentieth century rivers such as the Logan, Weber and Provo, draining west from the Wasatch Range, held huge populations of stoneflies of all species and therefore had healthy trout populations. Only remnants remain because of the ravages of development. In any case it is likely that the Mormon Girl originated here in those times of plenty and was created to imitate the adults of the smaller stonefly species. However, "Mormon Girl" has come to mean a specific combination of materials as has the "Royal Coachman." Specifically the Mormon Girl has a yellow body, red butt and speckled mallard flank wing or tail, and there is a range of Mormon Girl dry flies. One local variation is Hazel Hansen's Blond Mormon Girl which is tied like the described pattern but with ginger hackle and no tinsel rib.

As Ralph remembers, the Mormon Girl has been used for decades to imitate the adults of small stonefly species that emerge plentifully from many eastern Idaho streams. Typically these adults are lightly colored as is this pattern, although species with darker adults are also found. The red butt of the Mormon Girl imitates the egg sac of the ovipositing female which is very available to trout as it floats or skitters on the surface of rifles and runs. Thus it is over these stream features that this pattern will be most effective when dead drifted or skittered.

NEIL'S STONEFLY

Hook: *Mustad 3665A or equivalent, sizes 2-6.*
Thread: *Fluorescent orange monocord, 3/0.*
Body: *Fluorescent orange monocord.*
Rib: *Clipped brown saddle hackle palmered over body.*
Wing: *Dark or light elk body hair,* tied upright with wraps of thread at rear of wing.
Collar: *Clipped antelope hair finished with head cement.*
Head: *Antelope body hair spun then clipped to shape and finished with head cement.*

In any area where fly fishing is practiced there is a tradition of fishing and tying patterns which simulate major food forms that are specific to that area. And so it is in eastern Idaho with the giant and golden stoneflies, both historically present in most area streams. They still occupy many area streams in vast quantities, and for their nymph and adult stages there are many original and effective locally conceived patterns.

Neil Komoda, by profession a pharmacist and by passion a fly fisher, operates a well stocked fly fishing and fly tying department at B & B Pharmacy in Idaho Falls. With over 20 years of experience fishing area streams Neil has become a truly knowledgeable angler. Combining this experience with accomplished fly tying skills he has created a number of effective patterns for area waters. His dry stonefly, created in the early 1980s, is an excellent example and has taken many large trout.

Perhaps the most vulnerable time for adult stoneflies is during mating and egg laying activities when they frequently land heavily on the stream surface and flutter their wings while floating in the current attempting to escape. These activities attract even the largest of trout and for those fly fishers fortunate enough to encounter them, superb fly fishing results. Neil's Stonefly, with its upraised wing, was specifically designed to simulate a stonefly fluttering on the surface. But during egg laying flights it is one of the most effective patterns available, whether dead drifted or skittered over the surface. The spun, then trimmed, antelope hair head and collar give the fly excellent floating qualities and the raised wing, whether formed from light or dark elk body hair, makes the pattern highly visible and simulates the fluttering wings of the natural insect.

SOFA PILLOW

Hook: *Mustad 9672 or equivalent, sizes 4-8.*
Thread: *Black monocord, 3/0.*
Tail: *Red goose quill for brown version, yellow for gray version.*
Body: *Red floss or yarn for brown version, yellow floss or yarn for gray version.*
Wing: *Trude style: Red squirrel tail for brown version, gray squirrel tail for gray version.*
Hackle: *Three quality saddle hackles: brown for brown version, grizzly for the gray.*

Pat and Sig Barnes are among the finest and most loved personalities in fly fishing. For decades (until 1982) they operated the Pat Barnes Tackle Shop in West Yellowstone and offered quality products, gracious service and honest information to anglers and fly tiers alike. One of the most memorable and unique sights at their business was Sig tying flies on her foot powered sewing machine. The flies she produced were called, as were all produced in their shop, "Waterborn Flies." They were unexcelled in quality and effectiveness. Among these was the Sofa Pillow which they originated in the late 1940s to simulate adult giant and golden stoneflies. Tied Trude style with a squirrel tail downwing and brightly colored body, the Sofa Pillow is designed for floatability and visibility. Thus it is more heavily hackled than the classic Trude patterns with as many as four saddle hackles used in its construction.

In eastern Idaho two major variations of the Sofa Pillow are commonly used by float and bank fly fishers to simulate giant and golden stonefly adults. These are the brown version tied with a wing of red squirrel tail, red floss body, red goose quill segment tail and brown saddle hackle, and the gray version tied with a wing of gray squirrel tail, yellow floss body, yellow goose quill segment tail and mixed brown and grizzly saddle hackles. They are fished dead drift or skittered through riffles, runs and other fast water to simulate drifting adults and egg laying actions by females.

STAN'S WILLOW FLY

Hook: *Mustad 7957B or equivalent, sizes 10-16.*
Thread: *Monocord color to match natural insect, 3/0.*
Tail: *None.*
Body: *Tying thread of color to match natural insect.*
Wing: *Bunch of light elk hair.*
Hackle: *One grizzly and one brown.*

This is another of Stan Yamamura's creations and along with Stan's Hopper one of his most effective. Stan created this pattern in the mid 1960s to simulate the small stoneflies of which various species emerge from spring through autumn in many east Idaho waters. Because there was a strong demand for this type of fly, Stan made his Willow Fly so that it could be tied quickly with readily available materials. Elk hair is in good supply in east Idaho, and Stan raised roosters to provide hackles of all shades for his fly tying business. In addition to being a very effective stonefly pattern, east Idaho anglers soon discovered that Stan's Willow Fly was also a very effective adult caddis pattern on all waters throughout the season. By the early 1970s it had become the most popular adult caddis pattern fished on east Idaho waters. It retains its popularity to the present day but shares the spotlight with the more recently introduced Elk Hair Caddis and other adult caddis patterns.

Stan's Willow Fly is as easily tied as the locally popular variation of the Elk Hair Caddis which is also described in this book. The Willow Fly is equivalent to the Elk Hair Caddis in all respects including durability, versatility and effectiveness. Thus it will continue to be a local favorite. Its colors can be varied simply by using tying thread, dyed elk hair and dyed hackle to match the caddis species on which trout are feeding.

TRUDE

Hook: *Mustad 94840 or equivalent, size 6-12.*
Thread: *Black nylon, 3/0.*
Tail: *Reddish-brown hackle fibers.*
Body: *Scarlet wool yarn.*

Rib: *Silver tinsel.*
Wing: *Red fox squirrel tail.*
Hackle: *Two reddish brown neck or saddle hackles.*

The story of how Carter Harrison created this fly in 1901 at the Trude family's Algenia Ranch as a practical joke on A. S. Trude is well known in Island Park fishing lore. This practical joke, however, turned out to be not only a very effective fly for the Trude family and their guests, but also the forerunner of a style of tying. To many tiers the style of winging dry flies known as "down wing" is also known as "Trude style wing." Typically hair is used to form this wing which is tied down over the top of and parallel to the shank and no longer than the hook bend.

These flies are also hackled in front of the wing. The Trude Humpy, Trude Irresistible, Rio Grande Trude and Royal Trude are among these types. Charlie Brooks describes in *The Henry's Fork* how the Trude evolved in 1936 into Vint Johnson's Vint's Special. The fly was tied on a long shank hook, had a body of red silk floss and the same hackle, ribbing, tail and wing as the Trude. It became a very popular streamer and adult stonefly pattern on the streams of southwestern Montana, Yellowstone National Park and Idaho's Island Park area. Other well know patterns that incorporate the Trude style fox squirrel tail wing include the Picket Pin, Bloody Butcher and Sofa Pillow. Carter Harrison surely started something in fly tying with his turn of the century practical joke.

YELLOW SALLY

Hook: *Mustad 7957B or equivalent, sizes 12-16.*
Thread: *Yellow monocord, 3/0.*
Egg Sac: *Red tying thread.*
Body: *Lemon athletic bandage underwrap.*
Wing: *Coastal deer hair tied down-*

wing with tips extending just past bend.
Thorax: *Lemon colored dubbing.*
Hackle: *Three turns light cream neck palmered over dubbed thorax and wing.*

Locally, "Yellow Sally" is a collective name for the small stoneflies which are mainly members of the *Isoperla* and *Alloperla* genera. Many of these species are present in eastern Idaho, and they emerge throughout the season from quality water streams. On the South Fork of the Snake River, yellow sallies emerge from early season, when the river is carrying a combination of runoff and increased flow to satisfy downstream irrigation demands, through September when it is usually at its base flow. It is in this later season, after the larger stoneflies have emerged, that more attention is given to the yellow sallies on not only the South Fork, but other area streams. Locally, however, specific yellow sally patterns are not as widely used to simulate small stoneflies. Patterns like the Elk Hair Caddis and Stan's Willow Fly are more commonly used.

One specific pattern that is used for this purpose, however, is Bill Fuger's Yellow Sally. Bill, now retired and living in Idaho Falls, has been tying flies for decades and specializes in filling custom orders. He started tying this beautifully proportioned pattern in 1988. At first glance it appears to be a dry version for the Mormon Girl (*Isoperla mormoni*) but it is effective for all Yellow Sallies. An ability to conceive not only effective patterns but those of exact proportions and balanced construction established this gentleman tier as contributor to the art of fly tying.

Fished in larger streams such as the South or Henry's Forks of the Snake River, Bill's Yellow Sally is deadly when drifted through riffles or near overhangs. On smaller, steeper gradient streams it is effective when floated just about anywhere.

TERRESTRIALS

BING'S HOPPER

Hook: *Mustad 7957B or equivalent, size 12.*
Thread: *Tan nylon, 2/0.*
Beam: *To form extended body: Three fibers monofilament 0.006" diam.*
Rib: *Fine gold tinsel.*
Body: *Strip 3/8" wide, cut from athletic bandage foam underwrap.*

Rear Legs: *Pheasant tail segment (knotted to form joint).*
Underwing: *Polar bear dyed fluorescent orange.*
Wing: *Wood duck flank cut to shape, tied downwing.*
Front Legs: *Rock chuck tail fibers.*
Thorax: *Spun antelope clipped to shape.*

In eastern Idaho, this pattern is the most widely used of Bing Lempke's creations. For conceiving patterns such as this Bing, in 1988, won the Buszek Award from the Federation of Fly Fishers. The evolution of this hopper began in the late 1970s, as Bing, ever the experimenter and innovator, investigated various materials and configurations in the vise and on the stream.

It is fascinating to hear his story of combining materials and techniques to create this eminently effective and unique hopper pattern. In this evolution Bing chose antelope hair to form the head because of its superior buoyancy and spinning qualities. He used rock chuck tail fibers to form the front legs because of its reflection qualities and durability and dyed polar bear hair for the underwing because of its superior translucence as well as durability. He used bandage underwrap, a closed cell synthetic, to form the body and to add buoyancy.

Placing the front legs to extend out of the thorax at an angle to the hook shank helps to stabilize the fly as it rides on the water, and the extended body not only gives the fly realism and artistic balance but seems to make it more attractive to fish.

Bing used 0.006" diameter monofilament to form the beam on which to build the extended body because it has more strength and durability than horsehair.

There are two major variations of Bing's Hopper. The South Fork version has a body constructed of ivory underwrap and the North Fork version has a body constructed of tan underwrap.

Both are equally and superbly attractive to fish. They are still extremely effective if one substitutes hackle fibers or bucktail for the underwing, deer hair for the head and thorax and squirrel tail for rock chuck tail to form the front legs.

BLUE RIBBON FOAM BEETLE

Hook: *Mustad 94840 or equivalent, sizes 12-18.*
Thread: *Black nylon, 6/0.*
Body: *Black Polycelon tied on hook shank then folded over toward front to form shellback after legs*
are tied in.
Legs: *Three dyed black elk body hairs or dark elk mane hairs.*
Head: *Trimmed end of Polycelon forming shellback.*

This pattern is named for one of the most complete fly fishing specialty shops anywhere; Blue Ribbon Flies of West Yellowstone, Montana. Craig and Jackie Mathews and John Juracek operate Blue Ribbon Flies and their Blue Ribbon Foam Beetle is becoming a favorite on east Idaho waters because of its simplicity, durability and effectiveness. Beetles may take a back seat to hoppers in popularity but there are times when they are at least as effective. Beetles are found on land adjacent to all water types. Thus from late July to early October, when terrestrial insects are at their population peaks, beetle patterns can be fished dead drifted on the surface of all area waters. Black patterns such as this are difficult to see on the surface of all water types. Thus Craig and John recommend tying in a piece of orange or pink yarn on top.

The Blue Ribbon Beetle is perhaps the easiest of all beetle patterns to tie. The principal material of construction is closed-cell foam marketed under the name of Polycelon. One end of a black Polycelon strip about two inches long and no more than a quarter of an inch wide, for a size 12 hook, is anchored to the shank with tying thread. Three dyed black elk body hairs are tied to the shank at a right angle just behind the eye, then clipped to length to form legs. The strip is folded over the shank toward the front and tied down just behind the eye to form a shellback. A small clump of pink or orange yarn is tied in here, and the strip is cut off to form

a head and the fly is finished. A description of this fly and others that are effective in the Yellowstone area are found in Craig and John's excellent book, *Fly Patterns of Yellowstone.*

BOB'S HOPPER

Hook: *Mustad 9672 or equivalent, sizes 6-10.*
Thread: *Cream monocord, 3/0.*
Body: *Orange, yellow or tan Ethafoam, can be extended about the length of the hook gape.*
Rib: *Tying thread.*
Underwing: *Orange doll hair.*
Legs: *Pintail duck flank sections.*
Wings and Head: *Deer body hair forming bullet head with tips forming wing.*

There is one point that many fly fishers overlook when selecting or tying hopper patterns: choosing a color that is appropriate for the insect at a given time in the season. To maintain protection, hoppers change color during the season to match that of their surroundings. Early season hoppers are greenish in color, then as grasses ripen and cure, hoppers change colors from yellow and oranges to tan in autumn.

Likewise the overall size of hoppers increases with time although small individuals are always present.

Bob Bean, tying since the 1950s, has incorporated this color change into his hopper which he first created in the mid 1950s.

Resourceful as ever, he uses a mix of native materials and synthetics to get the color and impression he believes appropriate for the season. These include mule deer body hair, pintail duck flank feathers, Ethafoam and doll hair of appropriate colors. Doll hair is found in hobby and art supply shops, and Bob is a leading proponent of using this material in both dry and wet flies. Local tiers are waiting for him to reveal his ideas on its use, particularly because many fly fishers call his hopper and other patterns their favorites.

Some local tiers have learned how to tie Bob's Hopper through the fly tying classes he conducts in Blackfoot. When he explains to those in his classes or even to his fishing companions the importance of size and color he passes on information that not only helps in catching fish but makes the difference when that big and cautious lunker considers your imitation!

EZ HOPPER

Hook: *Mustad 9671 or equivalent, size 10.*
Thread: *Black monocord, 3/0.*
Tail: *Yellowish tips from a small bunch of mule deer body hair.*
Body: *Dubbed from a blend of four parts gold Fly-Rite, one part yellow Antron and one part* beaver fur.
Rib: *Brown saddle palmer wrapped on body then clipped short.*
Underwing: *Bunch of red bucktail.*
Overwing: *Bunch of mule deer body hair.*
Head: *Spun from mule deer body hair then clipped to shape.*

During nearly 20 years Paul Bowen has been through the whole spectrum of fly tying experiences including initial discovery, commercial tying and wide recognition for creativity. Over these years this native of the Rexburg area has conceived effective patterns for caddisflies, mayflies, stoneflies, hoppers and midges. Certain patterns of his have become favorites of many local fly fishers. Paul's EZ Hopper, created about 10 years ago and properly named because of its simple construction, is one of these. But there are other aspects to this pattern that have lead to its regional acceptance. With durability also in mind Paul specifically created this pattern to be visible, not only on slower waters, but on faster waters such as the South Fork of the Snake River and its tributaries.

Good hopper populations are found in various streamside habitats that are well vegetated. The South Fork and its tributaries, for example, abound in riffles and runs bordered by brushy, grassy banks. During August and September when float and walk-in fly fishers turn from large stonefly patterns to hopper patterns the EZ Hopper becomes ideal to fish back toward banks which can host hoards of hoppers. With its high standing wing this pattern, whether dead drifted or twitched, is more easily observed on its course through rough water than low floating patterns designed for smooth waters. The reward of using this high rider, therefore, becomes more hooked fish.

Some creative and practical aspects of the EZ Hopper include Paul's use of a red bucktail underwing to simulate the reddish coloring on the legs of many area hoppers and the development and use of a dusty yellow dubbing for its body construction.

This shade of yellow is common not only on mid summer hoppers but also on some adult caddisflies. Effective modifications of the EZ Hopper include Steve Christensen's use of orange bucktail for the underwing and Paul Christensen's addition of rubber legs in the shape of an X just behind the head. This latter modification is known as the EZ-X.

HAIR MOUSE

Hook: *Mustad 37187 or equivalent, sizes 2-6.*
Thread: *Gray nylon, size A.*
Tail: *Piece of fly line, rubber hackle or chamois.*
Body and Head: *Spun deer hair* clipped to shape including head and ears.
Eyes: *Black beads cemented on head.*
Whiskers: *Pieces of two-pound test monofilament.*

The Hair Mouse has been fished from time immemorial. Its use on European waters to simulate voles goes at least as far back as the fifteenth century. Since then it has been rediscovered time after time, and it seems that every competent contemporary tier has his or her own version.

By far the most useful material for tying hair mice is hollow hair, mostly from caribou, mule deer or whitetail deer.

Flies constructed of these materials ride high on the water without dressing of any kind and are durable. Use of good spinning quality, hollow hair, makes construction simply an exercise in covering the hook shank. Clipping the hair to shape, including forming ears, is the most tedious part of construction. Little else is really necessary for construction materials, although most versions use other materials for ears, eyes, whiskers and a tail.

In eastern Idaho the Hair Mouse is used mainly by experienced anglers to tempt large, difficult fish. Thus relatively few fish are taken but in many cases their use results in the largest fish of the year for the fly fisher. Particularly good places to fish Hair Mice include beaver ponds, meadow streams, along steep banks or overhangs or the surface of deep holes. The best presentations are those which use the rod to make the mouse "swim" on the surface, or simply a dead drift. The resultant take is usually an explosive roll or a subtle inhalation in which the mouse simply disappears below the surface.

JOE'S HOPPER

Hook: *Mustad 9672, or equivalent, sizes 4-14.*
Thread: *Black monocord, 3/0.*
Tail: *Scarlet hackle fibers.*
Ribbing: *Brown saddle hackle with fibers trimmed off sides after* wrapped on body.
Body: *Yellow or orange poly yarn.*
Wings: *Brown turkey quill segment tied in on each side of shank.*
Hackle: *Mixed brown and grizzly saddles.*

The story of this pattern's origin as the Michigan Hopper and Joe Brooks' subsequent use and testimony of its effectiveness is well known. This universally popular creation is also the most used hopper pattern in eastern Idaho. Every retail fly fishing specialty store in the area carries it which is a tribute no other hopper pattern can claim. The hopper season in eastern Idaho begins on lower elevation waters, such as on the Snake River Plain, by early July and ends near the end of October. Higher elevation waters have shorter seasons which may be as limited as mid August to early September. In season, hoppers are available to trout on practically every stream in the area. Thus there is probably not a stream in the area where Joe's Hopper has not been used effectively.

During the hopper season a major usage question for the angler is one of size. Smaller sizes are effective throughout the season. Larger sizes are effective later in the season when more large hoppers are available. Smaller Joe's Hoppers (sizes 10-14) are also used locally to simulate adult caddisflies and small stoneflies. Large ones (size 4-8) are used to simulate big stoneflies. These usages are further tribute to the effectiveness of this pattern. Hopper patterns are fished dead drift or with a subtle twitch on the surface. Cast hoppers to rising fish or as a searching pattern near overhangs, banks, rocks, logs and other holding water.

PHIL'S HOPPER

Hook: *Mustad 9672 or equivalent, sizes 10-14.*
Thread: *Yellow monocord, 3/0.*
Body: *Yellow wool or poly yarn, use monofilament to form beam for extended body.*
Wing: *Pheasant "church window feather."*
Legs: *Pheasant tail segment knotted to form joint.*
Jughead and Collar: *Spun elk hair with natural tips extending to rear.*
Indicator: *Tuft of red wool tied in at back of bullet head.*
Antennae: *Monofilament.*

Phil Blomquist is one of eastern Idaho's most prolific commercial fly tiers. His creations and versions of traditional patterns are marketed from retail outlets in his hometown of Pocatello, the Swan Valley area of the South Fork of the Snake River and as far away as Pinedale, Wyoming. Many of his creations are becoming traditional fare in these areas.

Phil is also an up and coming writer and has contributed to books and outdoor magazines.

Based on turnover his hopper is the most popular of his creations. Phil has offered this pattern commercially for about four years and has used it and passed it on to fishing companions for even longer.

"I really enjoy fishing out of the way places and that means you will find me on small streams and mountain lakes a good deal of the time," he states. "I've also found that this hopper of mine does very well in these waters as well as on our more popular waters. Try it anywhere you fish hoppers and present it dead drift, skittered or with a twitch. It will do very well for you. Use black for all components and it becomes an excellent cricket. I added that piece of red yarn at the top and rear of the bullet head for visibility in tight places in small streams or sheltered areas."

Phil's interest in fishing small streams brings up a good point. Small streams, and eastern Idaho has an abundance, are excellent for sharpening your presentation skills. Accurate presentations are a premium here because the target area is smaller. Fish have relatively fewer chances for food than in larger streams, so they are more opportunistic, but by nature they are also more cautious. Thus the reward for a studied approach and an inconspicuous presence is a lot of hook-ups.

Tactics learned and used on small streams will improve your success on large streams.

STAN'S HOPPER

Hook: *Mustad 9672, or equivalent, sizes 4-10.*
Thread: *Black monocord, 3/0.*
Underbody: *Yellow or orange chenille.*
Overbody and Tail: *Bunch of deer hair oriented so that natural tips form the tail. Overbody and underbody are secured together by spiral wraps of tying thread.*
Wings: *Matched turkey quill segments.*
Hackle: *Two grizzly and one brown saddle hackle.*

This fly is Stan Yamamura's most successful and well known creation. Stan tied flies commercially out of Idaho Falls, Idaho in the 1960s and 1970s and called his business "Stan's Flies." He created his hopper in the 1960s, and during this time he and his tiers produced it, along with other patterns, by the thousands to supply retail outlets and custom orders for individuals. Stan's Hopper remains in local use today and is as effective as other hopper patterns described in this book.

In fact, its versatility is such that during the season of giant and golden stonefly emergence local fly fishers still use it to simulate floating adults.

Stan's Hopper resembles a Joe's Hopper but there is a major construction difference in that Stan created his hopper with a bunch of deer hair tied in along the top of the body to provide added buoyancy and a wide platform on which to mount turkey quill segment wings. This bunch is secured to the chenille body with firm spiral wraps of tying thread, first to the rear, and then forward. The natural tips of hair making up the bunch extend to the rear about one quarter the length of the shank to form the tail. On each side of the butts near the front of the fly the wings are tied in, and the space remaining to the eye is used to tie in the hackles and the finishing knot. A local variation is made by tying a lower tail section of scarlet hackle fibers, with tips extending to the rear, on top of the shank before constructing the body.

WET FLIES

ATTRACTORS

BITTON SPECIAL

Hook: *Mustad 3906 or equivalent,
    sizes 8-14.*
Thread: *Black monocord, 3/0.*
Body: *Fluorescent yellow yarn such
    as Danville Depth-Ray.*
Overbody: *Four or five peacock*
herls tied in shellback style.
Hackle: *Sparse, formed by spinning
    about two dozen deer body hairs
    at the head then tying back to ex-
    tend tips past the bend.*

"Heck, I've fished that fly of Dad's since I was 12 years old back in the 1950s!" Denny Bitton said in his usual gregarious manner. "Since then we've fished it all over, and it produces everywhere we try it."

Glen Bitton has fished eastern Idaho waters for several decades. From Big Lost River to the South Fork of the Snake River he can relate a lifetime of fly fishing experiences.

"Denny was about 12 years old when I took him up on the Portneuf above Whiskey Mike's one day. We went on upstream to what was called Utah Bridge in those days because tourists fished from it," Glen reminisced. "I showed him how to cast so his fly would drift downstream then twitch it just under the surface in waters where fish were holding. I then went upstream to fish when Denny let out a whoop. I went back to see him landing a rainbow of about 12 inches," he continued.

"It was his first trout. He caught it on a Bitton Special and he's been hooked ever since," Glen smiled.

Like all attractors the Bitton Special simulates nothing in particular—its general buggyness tricks trout into taking.

The Bittons and their fishing companions present it in a number of ways, including the one that worked years ago for Denny.

Now this fly not only brings back memories to a family with a fly fishing tradition, but attracts trout wherever it is presented in eastern Idaho.

BOYLE'S SHRIMP

Hook: *Mustad 3399A, 3906B or
    equivalent, sizes 6-10.*
Thread: *Yellow monocord, 3/0.*
Tail: *Dyed orange bucktail with*
natural tips cut away.
Underbody: *Cream poly yarn.*
Shellback: *Cream poly yarn.*
Hackle: *White saddle.*

In recent years it has become common knowledge that throughout the season the reach just below Palisades Dam on the South Fork of the Snake River is an unparalleled holding area for very large brown and cutthroat trout. There are many theories as to why fish congregate here, and there are an equal number of approaches to fishing this area. Fly fishing is one of these approaches but the most effective way of presenting flies is on spinning gear and with heavy weights to get to the bottom of the deep, heavy water. In this way flies are dead drifted along the bottom, and when their rate of movement changes the hook is set. Flies that seem to be most effective when presented in this manner are light or brightly colored wet attractor patterns. These can also be presented with some success on traditional fly fishing gear by adding lengths of lead core trolling line to the leader to bring the fly closer to the bottom.

One of the flies that has been successful when fished in this manner with either spin or fly fishing gear is Kathy Radford's Boyle's Shrimp. Kathy and her husband Kevin live in Ririe, Idaho and have gained renown for tying durable and effective flies. Kathy created her shrimp pattern in 1987 and named it after a long time customer. Since its introduction it has fooled some very large trout in the waters below Palisades Dam. Anglers are now using Boyle's Shrimp on the Salmon River in central Idaho where it is proving to be an effective steelhead pattern.

CANADIAN RED LEECH

Hook: *Mustad 9672, 79580 or
    equivalent, sizes 4-10.*
Thread: *Black monocord, 3/0.*
Tail: *Dark purple, light purple or*
black marabou fibers.
Body: *Finished thin with yarn sold as
    "Canadian Red Leech" yarn or
    "Blood Leech" yarn.*

When a fly pattern is effective throughout the season it gains notice. Such is the case with the Canadian Red Leech which has become a mainstay on Henry's Lake.

Bill Schiess, the renown Henry's Lake angler who operates the tackle shop BS Flies just east of Henry's Lake, has written a book, *Fishing Henry's Lake*, in which he defines his fly fishing strategy. Guess which fly is mentioned the most?

That's right, the Canadian Red Leech! By the way, since publishing his book in 1988 Bill has developed the BS series of flies which is also proving to be very effective on Henry's Lake.

The Canadian Red Leech is named for the reddish purple variegated mohair yarn made in Canada that forms its body. The same yarn in brown makes the Canadian Brown Leech and in green the Canadian Green

Leech. All three of these are fished in different manners at different locations and times of the season. Consult Bill's book for details.

The Canadian Red Leach is being discovered as a producer on lakes, impoundments, beaver ponds and slow moving streams in eastern Idaho. I have used it effectively on Aldous Lake, beaver ponds in the Willow Creek drainage and on private impoundments on spring creeks above American Falls Reservoir. For my personal version I add a few strands of pearlescent Flashabou or Krystal Flash to the marabou tail.

FIZZLER

Hook: *Mustad 9671 or equivalent, sizes 4-12.*
Thread: *Black monocord, 3/0.*
Tail: *Orange duck or goose quill segment.*
Body: *Black, brown, gray or green chenille.*
Underbody: *Orange, red or yellow chenille.*
Hackle: *Brown or grizzly saddle hackle.*

For decades the Radford family of Ririe, Idaho has had a fly tying tradition. Kevin and his father Etsel specialize in creating flies for fishing the South Fork of the Snake River.

Over the years they have supplied their creations to retail outlets in the area. Many of these effective and durable creations have become so popular that Kevin and his wife Kathy have had to turn out thousands of dozens of flies each year.

Etsel, now deceased, created the Fizzler in the mid 1940s, and it has become perhaps their most successful pattern.

Not to be confused with the Fizzle, one of Franz Potts' series of woven body flies, the Fizzler is a constructive variation of the Woolly Worm. Kevin and Kathy have added effective variations and their Fizzlers are now tied in all combinations of black, brown, green and gray chenille bodies; orange, yellow or red underbodies, and palmered brown or grizzly hackle. To construct the Fizzler the Radfords first tie in the tail and a strip of yellow, orange or red chenille onto the bottom of the shank along with a length of tying thread and a brown or grizzly hackle. Next they form the body by covering the shank with another strip of brown, black, gray or green chenille and then tie in the lighter colored chenille to form the underbody. Finally they spiral the piece of tying thread over the fly, then hackle it. The result is the extremely tight and durable fly for which they are renown.

This wet attractor pattern is particularly effective when drifted through riffles using a sink-tip line.

GLO-BUG

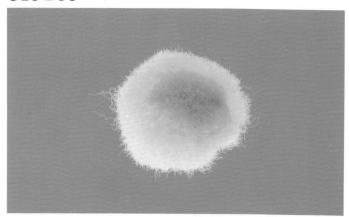

Hook: *Mustad 9174 or equivalent, sizes 4-8.*
Thread: *White monocord, Size A.*
Tail: *Optional, gold floss.*
Body: *Three one-inch long pieces of Glo-Bug yarn tied in tightly at center of shank, then pulled upward and clipped to shape.*

"Hell, if you are going to fish those things, you may as well be fishing salmon eggs!" Wes growled at me after he came down the river to watch me release the rainbow that had jumped several times thus catching his attention. "I'll be glad to buy you some to use, if you like. Then you could spend your tying time making up some real flies!" he grinned. His opinion may be shared by many fly fishers, but all of them, including Wes will not deny the effectiveness of Glo-Bugs. Originally created for steelhead and salmon in northern California, they have caught on around the globe and hook many different types of fish species.

Sensitivity in detecting a strike is important when using Glo-Bugs, making the use of a floating line, long leader and strike indicator most suitable. This assemblage is dead drifted through the water with the Glo-Bug close to bottom. As water being fished progressively increases in depth more weight should be added to keep the Glo-Bug drifting near bottom. An effective way of doing this is by adding lengths of lead core trolling line between the tippet and butt sections of the leader. Any movement of the indicator against the current flow means the hook should be set. Many times the result is a snag but there also can be an explosive response by a large fish.

In tying Glo-Bugs a couple of considerations are appropriate. Use only high quality, sharp scissors and keep the thread and yarn under positive tension during all tying and cutting operations. Securing yarn on the hook can be enhanced by applying a small drop of Superglue to the thread wrapped shank.

MITE SERIES

Hook: *Mustad 3906B or equivalent, sizes 8-14.*
Thread: *Black monocord, 3/0.*
Body: *Horse mane woven with floss underbelly using the Pott weave. Use white mane and yellow floss for Lady Mite, sandy mane and orange floss for Sandy Mite.*

Hackle: *Horse mane used to form body is tied back over body using thread wraps at the head of the fly. Cut ends such that tips extend just past hook bend.*

"If ya ain't gonna use worms, use a Sandy Mite!" cried the beer drinking cowboy as he drove a rattletrap pickup toward the setting sun. We had just informed him of our lack of success while fishing beaver ponds on Squirrel Creek east of Ashton, Idaho. It was likely that this son of the West was just a once-in-a-while fly fisher, but as with most area anglers he knew of the Sandy Mite. Franz Pott originated the woven hair Mite series in the 1920s from his tying operations in Missoula, Montana. The use of the Mite series spread throughout the West with the Sandy and Lady Mite becoming the most popular representative everywhere including eastern Idaho where they are used as all purpose nymphs. George Grant states in his masterpieces, *Montana Trout Flies* and *The Master Fly Weaver* that Pott originally used light sandy ox hair to weave the body and hackle of this fly. In eastern Idaho sandy horse mane is substituted for light ox hair. In his books Grant also describes the Pott weave, which links hair and floss to form the body, and how the fly is hackled by tying the butt ends of the horse mane back over the body to extend to the rear.

Joe Kortum Sr., who lived in Pocatello, was for years the premier eastern Idaho tier of the Mite series. Joe's Lady Mite is pictured above. His Lady Mites, Sandy Mites and Fizzles were used in waters from southwestern Montana to eastern Idaho and western Wyoming. Ace Shinderling's Mackay Special, in which a grizzly or brown hackle is tied in first, then palmered over the completed body, is a popular Sandy Mite variation used in eastern Idaho. It is named for the town of Mackay which is adjacent to the Big Lost River where Ace's fly was probably first fished.

NOBACK

Hook: *Mustad 9672 or equivalent, sizes 4-12.*
Thread: *Black monocord, 3/0.*
Body: *Weighted with turns of lead wire, or unweighted. Formed of peacock herl fibers spiralled around tying thread.*
Hackle: *Brown or ginger saddle.*
Rib: *Gold or silver wire.*

Since 1973 the Upper Snake River Chapter of Trout Unlimited in Idaho Falls has offered fly tying classes to the public.

These classes are offered on beginning and advanced levels by club members and emphasize instruction of locally effective patterns. The Noback, like many featured in this book, is one of the patterns discussed in these classes. The origin of the Noback is somewhat obscure. It was probably conceived almost simultaneously in a number of places, a fairly common occurrence in the origin of relatively simple patterns. The Noback has, after all, a simple and universally used predecessor, the Woolly Worm. It is also common knowledge in the art of fly tying that peacock herl is one of the most effective natural materials that can be used to attract fish to strike a fly. Thus the idea of a Woolly Worm having a peacock herl body could have occurred easily to many tiers almost simultaneously. And what an effective and versatile fly it is!

It can be tied in sizes to simulate nymphs ranging from mayflies and stoneflies to dragonflies and damselflies as well as caddis pupae and cranefly larvae. It is effective when dead drifted or twitched on a floating or sink-ing line. The food forms it simulates are found in still and moving water. It is exceptionally rugged, particularly if one takes care to spiral the peacock herl around the tying thread then form the body with this combination, and if one tightly counter-wraps over the hackled fly with thin gold wire. The choice of hackle color for the Noback is unlimited, but shades of ginger, brown and badger seem to make it most effective.

SAGWAH

Hook: *Mustad 7957B or equivalent.*
Thread: *Black monocord, 3/0.*
Tail: *Scarlet yarn.*
Rear Hackle: *Brown, sparse.*
Body: *Gray chenille.*
Front Hackle: *Grizzly, sparse.*

Darrel "Doc" Lindsay has lived in the Soda Springs area since 1949. During this time he has accumulated almost unequalled fly fishing experience on area streams. One of his favorites is the nearby Blackfoot River, one of the best cutthroat trout fisheries on the face of the earth. Doc conceived his Sagwah during the 1955 and 1956 seasons and named it after a fishing buddy known as "Chief Sagwah." Tales of "The Chief's" fishing prowess are local legends.

Originally Doc fished this fore and aft pattern on the Blackfoot as a wet attractor pattern to simulate an insect in distress. It was also effective in the murky waters of early spring on many area streams and when fished as a dropper with a Renegade or Gold Ribbed Hare's Ear on top.

Over the years use of the Sagwah has spread to other waters of eastern Idaho and to those in western Wyoming and northern Utah. Doc also believes that his fly is more effective on larger streams such as the Bear and Blackfoot rivers when tied with darker gray chenille. On smaller streams he believes that light gray chenille produces a more effective pattern. He prefers to tie his Sagwah on hook sizes 6 and 8, but finds that sizes 4 through 10 are effective.

Easy to tie, effective and durable, it is not difficult to see why this pattern is a success story. Following the development of a pattern is intriguing. If one looks at locales throughout the continent regional favorites such as the Sagwah are found, and a few eventually gain national popularity.

SOFT HACKLED FLY

Hook: *Mustad 94840 or equivalent, sizes 10-20.*
Thread: *Pearsall's orange silk or orange monocord.*
Body: *Cover shank with one layer of tying thread.*
Thorax: *Optional, single pheasant tail fiber or peacock herl.*
Hackle: *One or two turns of specked brown partridge or grouse feather.*

The Soft Hackled Fly is at least as old as the earliest chronicles of fly fishing. Dame Juliana Berners discusses them in her *Treatise on Fishing With a Hook*, dated 1496. In Europe these flies have been used to attract not only trout, grayling and whitefish but also salmon and rough fish. Many books dating from Berners' time to the present describe their use. The standard modern treatment of the Soft Hackled Fly are the three valuable volumes *The Soft Hackled Fly*, *Soft Hackled Fly Addict* and *Soft Hackled Fly Imitations* by Sylvester Nemes. In these books one will find a complete discussion on the use and construction of this superb type of fly whose basic character has not changed in nearly five centuries. It is no wonder that these are called the most effective wet flies conceived.

Soft Hackled Flies, sometimes called spiders, are most commonly used in eastern Idaho as caddisfly or mayfly emergers.

Fished in this manner the pattern is dead drifted just under the surface with a floating line and long leader to the area where emergers are being taken, then it is twitched or lifted to the surface with the rod tip.

The variety of soft hackled flies is endless, but as in other areas the partridge and orange pattern, listed above, is popular in eastern Idaho. Others include partridge and olive and partridge and yellow. All can be tied either with or without a rib, peacock herl or pheasant tail fiber thorax. It is most important to tie soft hackled files sparsely, with just enough tying thread to cover the hook shank. Not more than two turns of hackle should be used. Silk thread gives the body of these flies a translucent quality when wet and thus improves their effectiveness.

SUPER RENEGADE

Hook: *Mustad 9672, 79580 or equivalent, sizes 4-10.*
Thread: *Black monocord, 3/0.*
Tip: *Gold mylar*
Rear Hackle: *Grizzly or brown saddle.*
Rear Body: *Chenille of black, olive, brown, yellow, white, orange, pink or red.*
Middle Hackle: *Grizzly or brown saddle not to match rear hackle.*
Front Body: *Peacock herl or chenille of colors given for rear body, but not to match.*
Front Hackle: *White saddle.*

This is a local creation and a very popular one at that. Ardell Jeppsen living near Ririe, Idaho created this fly while recuperating from polio in a local hospital during the winter of 1959-60. He originally called it the "Hooligan," but with public use it became the Super Renegade. The "Super," as it is locally known, remains an overwhelmingly popular pattern on the South Fork but its use has spread to other area streams such as Henry's Fork, Falls River and Teton River. Supers are most effective when fished on a sink-tip line and cast toward the bank, underneath brush and around sweepers, snags and submerged rocks. Of course the most effective way to do this is from a boat.

The ancestors of the Super Renegade are the Renegade and the Double Renegade. However, unlike the first patterns, chenille is used to form the body segments. Ardell's original creation was formed with white hackle at the front, a brown hackle in the middle and a grizzly hackle at the rear. The front body segment of the original was made of peacock herl, and the rear body segment was white chenille. Popular variations now are usually made with different colored body segments with the lighter color being in front. Some of these include orange and black, white and peacock green, yellow and peacock green and orange and brown. Supers made with pink and black body segments are tied with a white hackle in front, a black hackle in the middle, and a brown hackle at the rear. Supers tied on size 4 hooks are most popular. A basic variation that is gaining in popularity is Wes Newman's Super X in which the middle hackle is replaced by two strips of white rubber hackle tied in with figure-eight wraps to form a cross.

TETON QUEEN

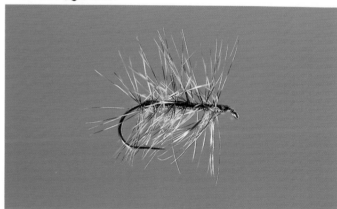

Hook: *Mustad 3399 A, size 10 for Teton Queen. Mustad 94840, size 12 or 14 for Teton King.*
Thread: *Black silk, 6/0.*
Body: *Black silk for both flies.*
Hackle: *Tied in tip first at bend and palmered over body; furnace for Teton Queen, grizzly for Teton King.*

TETON KING

Eastern Idaho's scenic centerpiece is Teton Valley. Streams from mountains on three sides combine with springs in the valley to form the Teton River. It is for the name of the river, the valley and the mountain range to the east that Leroy and Hazel Hansen named the Teton Fly Shop at their N5 Ranch just north of Tetonia. For years Hazel and her tiers supplied fly orders to the Carmichaels of Moose, Wyoming, to Glen Evans, Inc. of Caldwell, Idaho, to Buell Warner's South Fork Lodge in Swan Valley, Idaho and to the Kunz family at Alma's Lodge in Teton Valley. Then, about 25 years ago, Hazel created a fly that was to become very popular in eastern Idaho. She called it the Teton Queen.

"We used the Queen on any kind of water where fish were holding or feeding. We would cast it upstream and let it drift by us about three or four inches under the surface. As it rose to the surface fish would take it," Hazel recalled to me. "It fools a lot of fish and provides good times for lots of people."

The Teton Queen is an excellent all around emerger pattern. Soon after its effectiveness was proven Hazel produced the Teton King in which a grizzly hackle is palmered around the black silk body in place of the furnace hackle of the Teton Queen. The new fly was fished wet in the same manner as the Teton Queen. It was also found to be effective when fished dry to rising fish! The Teton King became a favorite of Bob Carmichael and became a sought after pattern in Jackson Hole.

Both patterns have the ingredients of popularity: simplicity, durability and effectiveness.

WHISKEY CREEK

Hook: *Mustad 7957B or equivalent, sizes 8-16.*
Thread: *Brown Coates and Clark two ply twisted sewing thread.*
Aft Hackle: *Soft white neck or sad-*
dle, slightly oversize.
Body: *Formed by a single layer of tying thread.*
Fore Hackle: *Soft brown neck or saddle slightly oversized.*

Soda Springs is sited in scenic country just south of a divide between the Bear and Blackfoot river drainages. In addition to these systems, within an hours drive of "Soda," one can also fish Willow Creek, Portneuf and Salt River drainages. This somewhat isolated community of just over 4,000 people has a tradition of fishing and with it many advocates of fly fishing.

There are notable fly tiers here who tend to favor their own creations over traditional patterns. A few of the local creations, however, are becoming area standards, and thus are stocked in local sporting goods stores. Perhaps the most popular of these is the Whiskey Creek created decades ago by O. S. Bybee. He named his classic fore and aft pattern after a Bear River tributary in southwestern Caribou County. Whiskey Creek has headwaters of such high quality that the Idaho Department of Fish and Game has operated a fish hatchery here for decades.

Bybee intended his fly to be an all purpose wet attractor for area streams of all sizes and in this role it has excelled.

Dead drifted or fished with a twitch in all moving water types it simulates a caddisfly pupa, mayfly emerger or diving insect.

In still waters it can be used to simulate mayfly emergers, caddisfly pupa, damselfly emergers and scuds. Along with its broad based effectiveness it has the other requirements for popularity: simplicity of construction and durability.

WOOLLY WORM

Hook: *Mustad 9672, 79580 or equivalent, sizes 2-12.*
Thread: *Monocord, 3/0, to match body color.*
Tail: *Optional: red or yellow yarn, short.*
Body: *Chenille: black is most popular, others colors include olive, brown, yellow or gray.*
Hackle: *Black, brown, grizzly or ginger saddle.*

Any discussion of popular western flies would be incomplete without including the Woolly Worm. One of the oldest patterns, it became a well known western fly in the early 1930s, because of the efforts of Don Martinez who heralded its effectiveness in the waters of southwestern Montana and Yellowstone National Park. Dark colored, weighted Woolly Worms fished wet successfully imitated the giant stonefly nymph. It remains as effective as ever for imitating the giant stonefly nymph even with the introduction of newer and usually more complex patterns.

The Woolly Worm must be considered a classic in simplicity, versatility and effectiveness. Tied in large sizes it imitates, in addition to stonefly nymphs, riffle beetle larvae, dragonfly nymphs and cranefly larvae. Tied in smaller sizes the Woolly Worm imitates damselfly nymphs, caddis pupa and mayfly nymphs. In eastern Idaho waters it is used to imitate all of these aquatic life forms and more. An example of its further use is to imitate a caterpillar species that is available to trout in the South Fork of the Snake River and its tributaries at the end of August and into September. This caterpillar is black with a central orange band, and Woolly Worm imitations are fished wet with floating lines near overhanging bushes and rock outcrops. Thus, the Woolly Worm remains a staple wet attractor pattern. Because the insects it simulates are always present in area streams, Woolly Worms in all colors should always be present in your fly box.

ZUG BUG

Hook: *Mustad 7957B or equivalent, sizes 8-16.*
Thread: *Black monocord, 3/0.*
Tail: *Tips from three peacock herls.*
Body: *Full, tied from peacock herls*
wrapped around tying thread.
Rib: *Gold or silver wire.*
Wing Case: *Short section of mallard flank.*
Hackle: *A few turns of soft brown.*

Like the Woolly Bugger and Henryville the Zug Bug is another famous Pennsylvania pattern. Cliff Zug is its originator, and as with the patterns mentioned above it has gained worldwide popularity.

"Boy, this river is just loaded with stiffies any more!" Denny Swanson said on his way up the gravel bar to see how I was doing.

"I've been using a number 14 Zug Bug and I've caught as many as I have rainbows," he continued. We had been fishing late season mayfly and caddisfly emergences on the Big Lost River above the town of Mackay. There had been action aplenty from rainbow and whitefish.

"Stiffie" or "Stiff" is local terminology for the mountain whitefish. This was my first exposure to the expression and, although amused, in my opinion whitefish provide good sport as well as excellent table fare. Action by whitefish helped make our day a fine experience as this distant cousin to the rainbow also took Gold Ribbed Hare's Ears and Pheasant Tail Nymphs with abandon. The Zug Bug, like the other flies mentioned, is an excellent pattern to use during concentrated emergences and for these periods is best fished dead drift or twitched along the surface with a floating line.

Weighted or unweighted it is also an excellent searching pattern for use on both floating and sinking lines in all water types. Traditionally it is tied with a silver oval tinsel rib counter-wrapped around the peacock herl body.

In eastern Idaho silver or brass wire are sometimes substituted for the oval tinsel. Use of wire results in a more tightly wrapped fly and thus increases durability.

NYMPHS

BITCH CREEK NYMPH

Hook: Mustad 9672, 79580 or equivalent, sizes 2-10.
Thread: Black monocord, 3/0.
Antennae and Tail: Two pieces of white rubber hackle for each.
Body: Black chenille on top, orange chenille on bottom woven using the parallel weave.
Thorax: Black chenille.
Hackle: Brown saddle hackle palmered over thorax.

Most fly fishers agree that this pattern probably originated in Montana, but there is a local faction that contends that it was named for the North Fork of the Teton River, which borders Pierre's Hole, as Teton Valley is also known, to the north.

The original name of this delightful-to-fish freestone stream is Bitch Creek. Its entire reach in Idaho forms the border between Teton County to the south and Fremont County to the north. Charlie Brooks relates some interesting facts on the naming of this stream in his absorbing book *The Henry's Fork*. There probably are Bitch Creeks in other western states as there are Elk, Sheep and Spring creeks. Flies are named after these creeks and thus become the sources of friendly debates and interesting discussions which add to the lore of fly fishing.

The Bitch Creek Nymph has been popular in eastern Idaho at least since the early 1960s. Since then it has been accepted as an eminently effective imitation of the giant stonefly nymph. Weighted and dead drifted deep through riffles and trout runs it produces trout and whitefish throughout the season. During times of giant stonefly emergence unweighted versions dead drifted or twitched slightly through riffles and near stream banks are very effective. Rubber hackle tails and antennae and soft saddle hackle add action. The most durable fly results from using the parallel weave to form the body from black and light orange chenille. A description of this weave can be found in Darrel Martin's superb book *Fly Tying Methods*.

BOX CANYON STONE

Hook: Mustad 9672, 79580 or equivalent, sizes 2-10.
Thread: Black nylon, 3/0 for larger flies, 6/0 nylon for smaller.
Tails: Two goose biots dyed dark brown.
Body: Fuzzy black yarn.
Wingcase: Brown turkey quill segment tied over the top of the thorax after hackle is wrapped.
Thorax: Fuzzy black yarn.
Hackle: Furnace saddle hackle palmered around thorax.

This pattern was created by Mims Barker of Ogden, Utah to simulate giant stonefly nymphs. The story of how this fly was developed in the early 1970s is outlined in Terry Hellekson's informative and valuable book, *Popular Fly Patterns*. Mims named the fly for the Box Canyon on the Henry's Fork. This canyon, located between Last Chance and Island Park Dam on the Henry's Fork, holds one of the densest populations of stoneflies found anywhere. It has thus become the standard by which stonefly waters and the effectiveness of patterns to simulate the nymphs and adults are measured. But there are excellent stonefly populations on other waters in eastern Idaho. An area that compares in density to that of the Box Canyon on the Henry's Fork is found in the higher gradient areas of the Blackfoot River above Blackfoot Reservoir. The use of the Box Canyon Stone is common here as well as in all area streams where giant stoneflies are found.

Tie the Box Canyon Stone weighted so that it can be dead drifted deep in runs throughout the season. Tie it unweighted for fishing in shallower waters, particularly along stream margins in periods of giant stonefly emergences. Twist the wool yarn used to form the body to give the fly a segmented effect. Locally, some fly fishers substitute tan yarn for black when using the Box Canyon Stone to simulate golden stonefly nymphs.

BRASSY NYMPH

Hook: Mustad 7957B, 3906 or equivalent, sizes 12-20.
Thread: Black nylon, 6/0.
Body: Close wrapped turns of brass or gold wire on rear two thirds of hook shank.
Thorax: Peacock herl fibers or ostrich herl in black, brown, olive or tan.

Most western states claim that one of its resident tiers originated this favorite. The bulk of the claims of origin come from Colorado and according to Terry Hellekson in his *Popular Fly Patterns*, credit goes to Gene Lynch of Colorado Springs. Regardless of the lore that links this fly to Colorado waters, it is popular and effective throughout the West. In eastern Idaho it is truly a pattern for year-round use. In winter it is an effective midge pupa pattern when used on open streams such as the South Fork of the Snake River downstream of Heise Hot Springs and Henry's Fork from Chester downstream.

It is also used throughout the general season as a midge pupa on streams, lakes and reservoirs. The Brassy Nymph's effectiveness cannot be denied but another reason for its popularity is simplicity. Easy to tie it has undergone many variations and its distinguishing feature is a body formed of malleable copper, or brass wire over a tapered thread base, which gives the fly a segmented and bright finish. In fact, there are commercial "Brassies" which are formed by close wrapping the entire hook shank with wire. Most variations, however, have a thorax constructed over the front third of the shank. In our area ostrich herl in black, brown, olive or tan, or peacock herl are commonly used for this purpose. The result is a durable fly.

BROOK'S MONTANA STONE

Hook: *Mustad 79580 or equivalent, sizes 4-8.*
Thread: *Black monocord, 3/0.*
Tail: *Six raven or crow primary fibers or pair of goose biots.*
Rib: *Copper wire.*
Body and Thorax: *Black fuzzy yarn.*
Hackle: *One grizzly saddle and another dyed brown, fibers stripped off lower sides then spiralled together in two turns over thorax.*
Gills: *Light gray ostrich herl wrapped at base of hackles.*

Charlie Brooks has made as many significant contributions to fly fishing in the last 40 years as anyone. We have all benefitted from his observations on trout behavior, on the physical and chemical nature of lakes and streams, on the food forms of trout and on the design of flies to simulate these forms. His generous expression of these observations in his books has enriched the literature of fly fishing.

Perhaps the most important food forms for trout in quickly flowing western streams are large stonefly nymphs. Realizing this, Charlie rigorously documented their behavior with many observations performed underwater. One critical point he emphasized in nearly all his books was that stonefly nymphs living in fast water, whether swimming or drifting, remain upright. Artificial flies, however, roll about their long axis when drifted through fast, turbulent waters. Thus his Montana Stone, which simulates the nymphs of the giant stoneflies, is symmetrical in construction about its long axis so that, even though it rolls in turbulent waters, it appears the same from all angles. Charlie noted that years of success with this nymph verifies his observations. He also heavily weighted his nymph and fished it on a sink tip line and short, stout leader to get it close to the bottom of the turbulent runs and riffles he enjoyed fishing. During his no nonsense delivery of the Montana Stone his fishing partners stood out of range.

When tying the Montana Stone particular attention should be paid to hackling. The two hackles used are first stripped of fibers on their lower sides then wrapped together. Afterwards ostrich herl is wrapped at the base of the hackle to simulate gills.

GIRDLE BUG

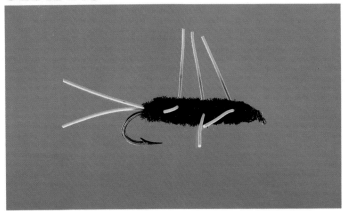

Hook: *Mustad 79580 or equivalent, sizes 4-8.*
Thread: *Black monocord, 3/0.*
Tail: *Rubber hackle pair, black or white.*
Legs: *Three pair rubber hackle tied in over lead wrapped shank.*
Body: *Black chenille wrapped after legs are tied in.*

The Girdle Bug has been popular throughout the mountain west and Pacific coast states for decades. Indeed, George Grant in his informative work *Montana Trout Flies* notes that although it came into popular use on the Beaverhead River in the mid 1960s it had been around for years before that. He also points out that the Rubber Legs and Girdle Bug are two discreet patterns. The former, he asserts, is tied on larger hooks, heavily weighted, constructed with black chenille and has tails and antennae made of goose biots. The latter is tied on hooks of all sizes and is not necessarily weighted. It is constructed with a variety of colors of chenille and has tails and antennae made of rubber hackle. The legs of both patterns are made of rubber hackle. Increasingly the name Girdle Bug, however, is being applied to both flies, and since the 1970s another variation, the Yuck Bug, has been gaining in popularity. When tying the Yuck Bug a saddle hackle of either brown, grizzly, ginger or badger is palmered over the shank of a Girdle Bug. All these variations of the Girdle Bug are fished wet by boat or tube anglers around sweepers, overhangs, submerged rocks and other cover throughout the season. In eastern Idaho an increasingly popular method is to fish them deep through riffles and runs of stonefly streams. Use a heavily weighted fly fished on a long leader and floating line with a strike indicator at the line-leader interface. The fly is drifted along the bottom within 30 feet of the angler and with the rod held parallel to the water's surface. Many times movement of the indicator against the current signals a strike. This method is deadly and can produce the largest fish of the year.

GOLD RIBBED HARE'S EAR

Hook: *Mustad 3906, 3906B or equivalent, sizes 6-16.*
Thread: *Brown monocord, 3/0.*
Tail: *Hare's mask guard hairs.*
Body: *Dubbed rough fur from base of ears and cheeks of hare's mask.*
Rib: *Fine gold wire.*
Legs: *Optional beard style hackle fibers.*

This is an all-time favorite nymph pattern. It probably originated on European waters but its effectiveness has resulted in world-wide use. Few nymph patterns have undergone as many variations as the Gold Ribbed Hare's Ear. Effective, easy to tie and durable are qualities that make it popular in eastern Idaho. It consists of a tail of hare's mask guard hairs, thin brass or copper wire ribbing and a tapered body of dyed olive, gold or natural dubbed hare's ear or mask hair. The tapered fly can be formed by overwrapping the dubbing in the thorax area or by weighting this area with close wraps of lead wire. Sparse or full flies can be made. With either, a rough or ragged surface seems most effective. This can be enhanced by picking out the finished fly with a dubbing needle.

Fished near the surface this pattern is a superb emerger in all water types and in a variety of stream gradients. Try dead drifting it no more than a foot or so beneath the surface to where fish are taking emerging insects. At this point lift the fly to the surface and prepare for action. This presentation is also effective for soft hackled patterns. Another effective presentation is dead drifting weighted or unweighted flies along the stream's bottom. Swing the fly down and across the current with a gradual lift or rhythmic twitches during retrieves in still water or slow moving streams.

GRAY NYMPH

Hook: Mustad 3906 or equivalent, sizes 6-18.
Thread: Gray monocord, 3/0.
Tail: Grizzly hackle fibers.

Body: Dubbed muskrat fur with soft, shaggy finish.
Hackle: A few turns of grizzly hen hackle.

"I'm 85 years old, and I've been retired for 70 of them!" said the crewcut gentleman with the ready smile as he answered my ring of his doorbell.

"So you want to know about my Gray Nymph? I created it in the 1930s. Clyde Ormond was so impressed with it that he wrote an article on it which appeared in Outdoor Life magazine back then."

This was Dee Vissing, a true outdoorsman and self employed inventor speaking. Dee has created several items for sportsmen over the years. His Gray Nymph is a constructive variation of the Muskrat Nymph which is still a popular pattern in eastern Idaho. As he discussed his nymph he was emphatic about what makes it effective.

"Tie it loosely!", he said as he picked one up and tossed it into a glass of water. Just like he explained the soft, pliant nymph in the glass reflected light from air bubbles trapped in folds of muskrat hair from which it was constructed.

"Most people wrap muskrat hair too tightly and it loses its ability to trap air and reflect light," he explained. "But if you wrap muskrat hair loosely as I do, you will have the fish- catchingest fly around. They are effective everywhere and in my 70 years of fly fishing I've fished them all over the West and some in the East."

I can't deny the logic of this pleasant and engaging man. My visit with him was in mid November when winter begins settling in on eastern Idaho. From that time on the Gray Nymphs that I have turned out have been the loosely wrapped versions that he advocates. And he is right; the soft finish has resulted in a much more effective fly.

MARCH BROWN NYMPH

Hook: Mustad 9671 or equivalent, sizes 10-14.
Thread: Orange nylon, 6/0.
Tails: Three pheasant tail fibers; tails are 2/3 the length of the hook shank.
Ribbing: Dark brown flat nylon.

Body and Thorax: Amber Australian opossum dubbing.
Wingcase: Dark turkey quill segment.
Legs: Speckled partridge feather fibers.

The term "March Brown" takes one back to times gone by in the British Isles. Originally, observant anglers there used it to describe mayflies emerging early in the season. Next "March Brown" was adopted by anglers such as Preston Jennings and Art Flick in the eastern United States to describe the early season Stenonema species of mayflies emerging from streams in New York's Catskill Mountains. The term "March Brown" is also used in the western United States. Rick Hafele and Dave Hughes use it in their landmark book Western Hatches to describe the early season emerging Rithrogenia morrisoni mayfly.

Bob Jacklin, the knowledgeable long-time fly fishing professional of West Yellowstone, Montana has also adopted the term. Bob, originally from New Jersey, guided in the early 1970s for Bud Lilly's Trout Shop before establishing his own business, Bob Jacklin's Fly Shop, in West Yellowstone in 1973. Over the years he has created many effective patterns for waters in Yellowstone National Park, southwestern Montana and Idaho's Island Park area. Bob's homage to "March Brown" is his March Brown Nymph which he developed on New York's Esopus River in 1970. He brought the nymph to West Yellowstone and it has gained proponents in, among other places, Island Park waters such as Last Chance, Harriman State Park and the Mack's Inn area. In these waters the March Brown Nymph can be used effectively to imitate early season mayfly nymphs and the golden stonefly nymph.

Bob uses a speckled Hungarian partridge body feather from which immature fibers are removed to form the legs on his March Brown Nymph, and he uses it in an uncommon but elegant manner. He ties the feather in by the tip, concave side up and butt to the rear on top of the anchor point of the wingcase. After the thorax is finished the butt end of the feather is brought forward and tied in just behind the hook eye. The wingcase is then brought forward and tied in at the same point. This fixes the downward curving feather fibers in place to simulate legs. The resulting symmetry of this nymph is superb but more important it is very effective in taking trout. Because of these aspects it is becoming a standard all-season nymph for eastern Idaho waters.

Montana Black Nymph

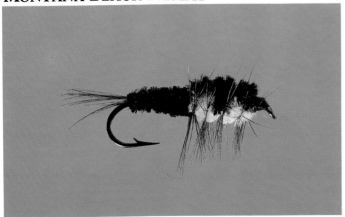

Hook: *Mustad 9672, 79580 or equivalent, sizes 2-10.*
Thread: *Black monocord, 3/0.*
Tail: *Pair of goose biots.*
Body: *Black chenille.*

Thorax: *Black chenille on top, yellow chenille on bottom woven with the parallel weave.*
Hackle: *Dyed black saddle hackle palmered over thorax.*

The origin of this pattern needs no further discussion. Information about its creator is quite scarce but it is easy to find opinions of its origin throughout Montana. This nymph pattern dates back to the 1940s and is a long time favorite for simulating the giant stonefly nymph, and as such is offered for sale in every fly fishing retail shop in eastern Idaho. The Montana Black Nymph has lost some of its popularity to the Bitch Creek Nymph and Box Canyon Stone. All of these patterns are in popular use throughout the season, but particularly during the giant stonefly emergence when they are all fished in the same manner and preference of one over another is usually a subjective matter.

Construction of the Montana Black Nymph is similar to that of the Bitch Creek Nymph except that the thorax is constructed of yellow chenille, whereas on the Bitch Creek Nymph the ventral surface of the body is constructed of orange chenille. When constructing the Montana Black Nymph the black chenille wing case and the yellow chenille used to form the thorax can be linked through use of the parallel weave as given by Darrel Martin in his book *Fly Tying Methods*. However, many tiers prefer to simply pull the excess from the piece of black chenille used to form the body over the hackled thorax to form the wing case. Variations for tailing this pattern include the use of a pair of goose biots, opposing brown saddle hackle tips placed with dull sides facing in, or brown hackle fibers.

Moss Caddis Emerger

Hook: *Mustad 7957B or equivalent, sizes 12-18.*
Thread: *Black nylon, 6/0.*
Body: *Woven by a succession of overhand knots using two pieces of embroidery floss each of single*

strand for smaller sizes, double or triple strand for larger.
Thorax: *Single peacock herl reinforced with tying thread.*
Hackle: *A few turns of speckled partridge.*

Many consider Scott Moss to be the master fly weaver of eastern Idaho. For 15 years this Idaho Falls resident has created patterns of outstanding effectiveness, durability and artistic quality. Scott ties these patterns for commercial resale and custom purchase as well as personal use. Such is the case with this pattern which he created in the mid 1980s for fishing the early season caddis emergence on Henry's Fork in the Chester/St. Anthony area. At first glance this emerger appears to be a traditional soft hackle fly with a full body. However, on observing the body one sees that it is woven by a series of overhand knots using embroidery floss to obtain a unique segmented effect.

Scott fishes his emerger dead drift at middle and shallow depths, and it produces most strikes as it arcs up in its swing to the surface in the area where fish are taking emergers. He also presents it on a deep, dead drift using a sink tip line of leader weighted with a split shot or length of lead core line. Again, the emerger produces strikes as it swings up from the bottom at the end of the drift. An emerger with a dark green back and bright green belly is most effective if one fishes the early season emergence on Henry's Fork. Orange and brown emergers are also effective in area streams when caddisflies of these colors are active. The pattern remains effective even when used to the point where most of the hackle fibers are missing.

Moss Stonefly Nymph

Hook: *Mustad 9672 or equivalent, sizes 4-8.*
Thread: *Black monocord, 3/0.*
Tails and Antennae: *Dyed black or brown goose biot pair.*
Underbody: *Art Foam underwrap to taper body.*

Body: *Two strands of four strand black wool tightly wrapped to obtain segmented effect.*
Thorax: *Tan Furry Foam.*
Hackle: *Soft furnace hackle tied in tip first.*
Wingcase: *Black Furry Foam.*

Large stonefly nymphs are the most important single trout food item in many eastern Idaho streams. In their natural state nearly all area streams historically held either golden or giant stonefly nymph populations or both. Thus it is not surprising that there is a long standing tradition of tying stonefly nymphs, and many local fly tiers who conceive their own patterns have versions of golden and giant stonefly nymphs. This Scott Moss pattern dates back to the early 1980s when he began tying it on a commercial basis for Ralph Alexander's Hackle Den, the first full service fly fishing retail shop in Idaho Falls. Scott conceived the pattern with durability and ease of tying in mind. At that time it outsold patterns such as the Box Canyon Stone, Montana Black Nymph and Bitch Creek Nymph in Ralph's shop.

It is still a big seller in the area, and Scott considers it to be the most effective of the patterns he has originated. It is fished along the bottom in waters hosting stonefly nymphs in the same manner as traditional stonefly nymph patterns. Scott prefers to fish his pattern soon after streams reach their base level after runoff through the first two weeks of the giant stonefly emergence. The pattern is tied on a hook shank that is bent about 15 degrees and weighted with lead wire wraps. Then Scott underwraps the body with Art Foam to give it an even taper. Next the body is tied over this tapered form by tightly wrapping two strands of four strand black wool yarn. Next the thorax is constructed. To give the fly natural action Scott hackles his pattern with a soft furnace saddle hackle which he ties in tip first. The wingcase is then tied in over the hackled thorax.

PHEASANT TAIL NYMPH

Hook: *Mustad 7957B, 3906 or equivalent, sizes 10-18.*
Thread: *Brown or olive nylon, 6/0.*
Tail: *Pheasant tail fibers.*
Body and Thorax Underwrap: *0.005" diam. copper wire.*
Rib: *Same as underwrap.*

Body: *Pheasant tail fibers.*
Thorax: *Peacock herl reinforced with tying thread.*
Wingcase: *Pheasant tail fibers.*
Legs: *Butt ends of pheasant tail fibers are used to form wingcase.*

The combined arts of fly fishing and fly tying are heralded in rich international literature. A significant work is Frank Sawyer's intense yet exquisite *Nymphs and the Trout*. This detailed work describes the interactions of trout and their major food form, mayfly nymphs, in British chalk streams. Reading this detailed book requires rigorous attention but the rewards in understanding the subject are many, for there is much significant fishing information which applies around the world. Among the gems in fly fishing is Sawyer's Pheasant Tail Nymph which he proposes for general use in simulating nymphs of many mayfly species in all water types. Thus in eastern Idaho the Pheasant Tail Nymph can be used to simulate a variety of mayfly nymphs. None other than Pat Barnes championed the Pheasant Tail Nymph for use in western waters of North America. Locally, Stan Yamamura advocated its use in area waters. Both Pat and Stan offered versions which were effective in all water types. Of course, both were also attracted to the Pheasant Tail Nymph for commercial reasons because of its ease of construction from readily available materials. They tied the nymph in all sizes from 10 to 18 and on hooks of various styles. Now it is a standard attractor nymph used throughout the region. But it is particularly effective as an emerger when twitched to the surface on a floating line and long leader. Used in such a manner it has been a long-time favorite in eastern Idaho.

PRINCE NYMPH

Hook: *Mustad 7957B or equivalent, sizes 8-16.*
Thread: *Black nylon, 3/0.*
Tails: *Pair of dyed brown goose biots.*

Rib: *Brass or silver wire.*
Body: *Peacock herl fibers twisted around tying thread.*
Hackle: *Brown neck or saddle.*
Horns: *Goose biot pair.*

Doug Prince of Monterey, California created this fly in the 1940s, and he originally called it the Brown Forked Tail. Buz Buszek renamed it the Prince Nymph. Doug, in 1981, became the twelfth recipient of the Buszek Award, the most prestigious in the art of fly tying. The Federation of Fly Fishers makes this award annually to the fly tier who has superior fly tying skills, has made original contributions to the art and who has a history of sharing knowledge through teaching and publication.

The Prince Nymph has become a standard all purpose nymph in eastern Idaho. Its popularity is now on a par with the Gold Ribbed Hare's Ear, Gray Nymph and Pheasant Tail Nymph. Tied weighted or unweighted it is most effectively fished dead drifted through riffles and runs, in toward banks or around obstructions. During emergences, bringing it to the surface at the end of a drift will attract fish. In still water it can be fished deep to simulate dragonfly nymphs or in shallower water as a damselfly emerger. When tying the Prince Nymph particular attention must be paid to placing the goose biot pairs which form the horns. These are tied in after the hackle, and the surface on which they are placed should be tapered with tying thread toward the hook eye. Placement of the horns on either side of the upper part of this surface will allow them to flare outward and slightly upward when tied in.

3 BAR X

Hook: *Mustad 9672 or equivalent, sizes 4-6.*
Thread: *Black nylon, size 2/0.*
Tail: *Forked, with a few strands of black horse mane hairs on each side.*
Underbody: *Orange yarn.*
Body: *Formed by parallel weave with dark sorrel horse mane on top, and tan sorrel horse mane on bot-*

tom. Use slightly more dark mane than tan.
Wing: *Red squirrel tail. Wing should extend to hook bend.*
Legs: *Black horse mane: tied such that the front pair angle forward and the back pair angle to the rear.*
Antennae: *Pair of black horse main hairs.*

Laurn ("Ash") and Elgarda Ashliman opened their retail business, Ashliman Shoe Store, in Rexburg in 1938. The business remained open for 38 years until June 5, 1976 when Teton Dam failed, flooding Rexburg and several nearby communities. But shoes were not the only merchandise the Ashlimans sold in their store.

"I started tying the 3 Bar X just after we opened the store. We sold it out of the store, and as it caught on people from all over the country came in to buy it, or they ordered it by mail. Why, over the years Elgarda tied it by the thousands," Laurn recalled.

"I appreciated tying that fly because in those days money wasn't easy to come by, especially for anyone like us trying to raise a family," Elgarda added.

"I first used the 3 Bar X in the rocky riffles and runs of the Box Canyon on the Henry's Fork. Right after the Second World War fishing was wonderful up there as gasoline rationing had prevented much travel. I used to bet my fishing partners, and any other taker, a dollar that I would catch a fish on my first cast with it. You know I never lost a bet. And that fly sure paid for a lot of my fishing trips!", he smiled. "We originally used Herter's Chinese squirrel tail for the wing of our fly. This tail has three dark bars, and along with the "X," taken from the way we tied in the dark horse hair legs, was the basis for its name. When China went Communist this squirrel tail became unavailable, so we substituted red squirrel tail for the wing. This tail has a single bar, thus people increasingly referred to our fly as the Bar X."

Three Bar X or Bar X, this is a fly of legend in eastern Idaho. From Laurn's original use in the Box Canyon it has been a superior imitation of the giant stonefly nymph on such eastern Idaho streams as the South Fork of the Snake River, Teton River and Falls River. In these waters it is fished through riffles and runs as Laurn first fished it years ago.

Its use, but not its effectiveness, has been surpassed by more quickly tied stonefly nymph imitations because performing the parallel weave with horse hair is time consuming. In fact, any 3 Bar X found today is a collector's item. Such is also the case with any Bar X tied by Laurn or Elgarda Ashilman.

VELOUR STONEFLY NYMPH

Hook: *Mustad 9672 or equivalent, sizes 4-6.*
Thread: *Black monocord, 3/0.*
Tail: *Pair of dyed brown goose biot.*
Underbody: *Tan Furry Foam.*
Body: *Black robe velour strip, 3/8" wide.*
Thorax: *Tan Furry Foam over lead wire wraps.*
Hackle: *Brown hen hackle.*
Wingcase: *Black robe velour strip, 1/2" wide.*
Antennae: *Black brush bristles.*

"Funny how realization that things can be used in fly tying comes to you. I was reading the paper one evening, six or seven years ago, and my wife Pat was sewing a robe. A piece of material she had finished working with was within reach, so I picked it up and noticed that it was elastic in one direction and not in the other. When I stretched it along that axis it also formed a tube.
"What is this stuff?", I asked her."

"It's robe velour, and I know what you're thinking!" Pat replied.

Thus Bill Fuger discovered the essential material with which to create his Velour Stonefly Nymph. Bill, a long time eastern Idaho tier, is renown for creating effective and durable patterns. To the experienced tier this account should be familiar and is one of the joys of fly tying. To many eastern Idaho fly fishers this nymph is preferred over standards such as the Bitch Creek Nymph, Box Canyon Stone or Montana Black Nymph when simulating the giant stonefly nymph. Bill forms the body of this nymph by first tying a 1/2" wide velour strip underside up, then wrapping the rear two-thirds of the shank with tan Furry Foam. He then brings the piece of velour over the top at the same time stretching it, and ties it in with the end of the Furry Foam in the manner of forming a wingcase. The thorax and wingcase are formed in the same manner, but before the wingcase is tied in a hen hackle is tied in by the tip and facing the rear. It is then folded over to the front and tied behind the hook eye. When the 1/2" wide piece of velour is tied in to form the wingcase the hen hackle is forced downward and is then lacquered to form three legs on each side.

STREAMERS

FALLS RIVER FLASHER

Weighted with leadwire wraps around the hook shank and dead drifted deep or stripped in with short pulls it is effective throughout the season. Unweighted versions fished closer to the surface in riffles or along banks, particularly by float fishermen during the golden and giant stonefly emergences, bring action. These emergences ascend lower Henry's Fork in late May and early June but occur in the Falls and Teton rivers in mid and late June because of heavier runoff loads.

The Falls River Flasher's simplicity of construction and its effectiveness come through the use of easy to work with materials which instill motion. These qualities have enhanced its popularity. The construction and materials listed above were given by Len Cattabriga of Victor, Idaho.

HORNBERG

Hook: *Mustad 9672, 79580 or equivalent, sizes 4-6.*
Thread: *Black monocord, 3/0.*
Tail: *Full, olive marabou as long as hook shank with two or three* *strands of rainbow crystal hair on either side.*
Body: *Medium olive chenille.*
Hackle: *Three or four turns of soft brown or dyed olive saddle.*

Falls River is an eastern Idaho rainbow trout fishery eclipsed only by the Henry's Fork. A healthy population of rainbow up to several pounds inhabits this stream which is a series of riffles, runs and deep holes. Because of these water types streamer patterns of all configurations are very effective. The Falls River Flasher, named for this stream, was developed locally and is gaining popularity in the waters of its namesake and in the Teton and Henry's Fork drainages.

Hook: Mustad 9672 or equivalent, sizes 2-10.
Thread: Black monocord, 3/0.
Body: Gold or silver sparkle braid or flat tinsel.
Underwing: Orange or yellow marabou.
Wing: Matched barred mallard flank feathers on sides.
Overwing: Three peacock herls.
Shoulder: Junglecock or orange or yellow marabou.
Hackle: Brown or furnace.

The Hornberg was conceived in the Midwest, and most sources credit its creation to Frank Hornberg. It was originally a wet fly and gained a reputation as being effective on brook trout in upper midwestern and Canadian waters. However, because of its reputation as an effective pattern, its use spread not only to other areas but also to that of a dry fly. As a smaller dry it becomes an effective caddis pattern; as a large dry it is an effective stonefly pattern. Presently in eastern Idaho it is undergoing rediscovery as an effective streamer pattern for lakes and streams. Floyd Fantelli of Idaho Falls, and Buck Goodrich of Shelley, have described modifications of the Hornberg which are effective in area lakes, beaver ponds and streams. An example of the fascinating discoveries that make fly tying and fly fishing so rewarding is that Buck and Floyd find that the Hornberg used as a streamer is particularly effective in the early season for fooling large brook trout in area lakes and beaver ponds. Effectiveness in the Midwest for catching brook trout is what gave the Hornberg popularity years ago! It is also effective when fished deep and slow in area rivers and lakes for cutthroat and rainbows. The main modification that Buck and Floyd impart to their version of the Hornberg is to use marabou fibers as an underwing rather than hackle tips or bucktail. They also optionally use marabou fibers in forming the shoulder of their version as described in the directions above.

MARABOU JUGHEAD

Hook: Mustad 79580, 3665A or equivalent, sizes 1-4.
Thread: Red monocord, Size A.
Body: Gold or silver sparkle braid reinforced with tying thread.
Weight: Split lead shot crimped on shank 1/8" behind eye.
Wing: Marabou bunches with strands of Flashabou or Krystal Flash.
Jughead and Collar: Spun hollow hair with natural tips extending to rear.

We have all encountered line drag which prevents our fly from getting down to the greatest stream depths where the largest fish hold. It's frustrating when you know the big guys are down there and your fly sails over them. Remembering back to my spin fishing days with bait and lures when split lead shot gained me depth, I came up with one solution to this frustration some years ago. I call it the Marabou Jughead, and it has proven to be a real producer that is catching on around the West. A split lead shot crimped onto the hook shank just behind the eye gets this fly down to the depths. But what makes it so effective is the action given to it by split lead shot up front and the wing formed of marabou fibers and a few strands of Flashabou or Krystal Flash. To big fish in deep water this fly, when fished properly, simulates an escaping minnow, a drifting leech or a drifting night crawler. The best way to fish the Marabou Jughead is to dead drift it into a deep run or hole, then as it reaches its greatest depth retrieve it with a jig-

ging action. Most hits occur during this retrieve but I have found that an occasional twitch during the dead drift also brings hits! And it is equally effective when fished with a jigging action in shallow or still water. All these presentations require heavier rods and lines, of course, but the rewards are strikes by the largest trout in the stream.

There are two critical operations in tying this fly. The first is to wind a layer of thread on the shank where the split lead shot is to be crimped. This layer secures the shot on the shank making it less likely to rotate. The second important operation is in forming the jughead of deer or elk hair over the crimped shot. This is best done by spinning deer hair onto the shank in front of the crimped shot and the hook eye. Then using a tool having an orifice of sufficient diameter, push the hook eye, then the spun hair into the orifice such that the hair envelopes the shot with the tips pointing to the rear.

Snug wraps of thread around the hair just behind the crimped shot and a whip finish at the same point will then form the jughead.

MARABOU MUDDLER

Hook: Mustad 9672, 79580 or equivalent, sizes 2-10.
Thread: Gray nylon, 2/0.
Body: Gold or silver sparkle braid.
Wing: Bunch of marabou: single color; black, brown, olive, orange, red, white or yellow; two colors any combination of the preceding with darker color on top.
Overwing: Three peacock herls.
Collar and Head: Spun deer hair with butts clipped to shape head.

This is another variation of the Muddler Minnow introduced by Dan Bailey. The Marabou Muddler is in worldwide use but is considered a western fly because of its creator and original use in Montana waters. In eastern Idaho it has a reputation as a big fish catcher and thus is usually fished in sizes larger than six. Wings of two colors are popular with the darker color forming the top half of the wing. A few strands of Flashabou or Krystal Flash are usually mixed with the marabou wing which is topped with a few peacock herls.

One of the best season long presentations of this fly is to drift large weighted versions on sink tip lines and short, heavy leaders into deep holes or undercuts or under sweepers or brush. As the fly begins to drag it is swung up and twitched with action from the rod tip. This results in strikes as the fly rises from close to the bottom and swings across the stream. Another effective use of this fly occurs during the autumn brown trout run in streams such as the South Fork of the Snake River, the Snake River and Salt River tributaries. In this presentation the unweighted fly, on either a sink tip or floating line, is swept across gravel bars where redds are found. The best gravel bars to fish at these times are those just above good holding water. Aggressive browns will fall for the Marabou Muddler if the fly fisher's approach to this water is refined.

MATUKA

Hook: *Mustad 79580 or equivalent, sizes 2-8.*
Thread: *Black monocord, 3/0.*
Body: *Yarn or floss of any of the following colors: black, brown, cream, gold, olive, orange, tan or yellow.*
Rib: *Gold or silver wire.*
Wing: *Two pair of saddle or large neck hackles mounted on shank, one pair per side with shiny sides out. Use brown, badger, grizzly or white in natural or dyed any color.*

"Matuka" is the distinctively native style of tying streamers in New Zealand. Now it has spread around the world to produce Matukas in a vast array of variations. The basic style produces an effective and durable fly simply by mounting pairs of large neck or saddle hackles horizontally along the body and securing them to the body with floss, thread or wire ribbing. The nuisance of hackle tips frequently wrapping around the hook bend results from a traditional style of hackling streamers by tying their butts in only at the head of the fly. The Matuka style of hackling steamers minimizes this occurrence. Matukas are easily tied, but there are two acts which must be performed with care during construction. First, hackles paired two for each side should be combined with all dull faces inward. Then all fibers on the bottom sides, except the portions forming the tail, should be removed by pulling toward the butt. Second, after the hackle butts have been tied in at the head of the fly the fibers are stroked forward. They are brought back in segments determined by the spacing of the ribbing wraps used to secure them to the body of the fly.

In eastern Idaho Matukas are fished in the manner of all streamers: on sinking lines in still water, and weighted or unweighted on floating and sinking lines in moving water.

Popular color combinations used in eastern Idaho are olive wing and body, black wing and body, badger and brown or grizzly wing with cream, red or brown body. A few wraps of soft hackle or a beard of hackle fibers is optional.

MICKEY FINN

Hook: *Mustad 9672, 79580 or equivalent, sizes 2-10.*
Thread: *Black monocord, 3/0.*
Body: *Flat or embossed tinsel.*
Rib: *Oval silver tinsel.*
Wing: *Small yellow section of bucktail topped with section of red bucktail of about same size topped by section of yellow bucktail as large as two lower sections combined.*

This classic bucktail streamer, originated by John Alden Knight, means different things to different east Idaho anglers.

Interestingly, bait fishermen here hook nightcrawlers onto Micky Finns and settle this combination on the bottoms of local lakes and reservoirs. Depending on your point of view, either fly fishing or bait fishing is sullied by this ritual!

Nevertheless, this combination has produced catches of large trout over the years. More conventionally the Mickey Finn has been used for decades in eastern Idaho for trolling by fly and spin fishermen alike. More recently advocates of these methods equipped with float tubes cast the Mickey Finn with good results. A more specific and perhaps classic use of this pattern is in tailwaters during autumn brown trout spawning runs. The pattern in large sizes (4-6/0) is a favorite below American Falls and Palisades dams during these times. Here large flies fished over gravel bars holding redds or deep in holding water consistently produce large browns.

Lead wire wraps around the hook shank can weight this fly. In this case sparkle braid is easiest to use to form the body. Tinsel is more appropriate to form the body on unweighted flies. Tie on the bucktail wing in three sections, first the yellow, then the red then the top yellow. Successively stagger the butts of each section a fraction of an inch to the rear to obtain a more evenly tapered and securely tied head. As a final touch consider painting eyes on the head.

MUDDLER MINNOW

Hook: *Mustad 9672, 79580 or equivalent, sizes 2-14.*
Thread: *Gray nylon size 2/0 to A depending on size of fly.*
Tail: *Turkey quill section.*
Body: *Flat or embossed silver or gold tinsel.*
Underwing: *Brown kiptail bunch.*
Wing: *Brown turkey quill sections tied in together, shiny sides out, on edge over body.*
Collar and Head: *Spun deer hair with butts clipped to shape to form head.*

There is an intriguing story about how George Washington Carmack and his Indian partners (while camping on a tributary of the Klondike River in quest of salmon to sell) made the discovery strike on August 16, 1896 which started the gold rush to the Yukon Territory. In a similar manner Don Gapen, with Indian guides, was camped on Ontario's Nipigon River in quest of world record brook trout. Here, 41 years later, almost to the day, Gapen created the Muddler Minnow. In a sense he too discovered gold with this conception which is one of the most versatile patterns ever created. Gapen's purpose for the fly, which he called Gapen's Fly, was to imitate local minnows to entice a world record brookie. He later renamed it the Muddler Minnow. As such it has been used not only for trout and steelhead, but bass, salmon and almost all other game fish in fresh and salt water. Dan Bailey changed the fly to its now popular configuration of a closely clipped bullet head of spun deer hair and a calf tail underwing in place of bear hair.

Bailey also derived the Marabou Muddler and the Spuddler from the Muddler Minnow, and all three became immensely popular in the North American west.

In eastern Idaho the Muddler Minnow is the most widely use fly for big fish. In moving water it is fished near the bottom to simulate local sculpin and nymph species. In still water with a sink tip or full sink line it is a superb baitfish pattern. As with its descendant the Dry Muddler, it is a superb searching pattern. In this use it is best fished on a sink tip or a floating line around undercut banks, rocks, sweepers and other types of cover where large fish are likely to hold.

SHEEP CREEK SPECIAL

Hook: *Mustad 9672, 79580 or equivalent, sizes 6-14.*
Thread: *Black monocord, 3/0.*
Hackle: *Sparse brown at hook bend.*

Body: *Olive chenille.*
Wing: *Speckled mallard flank, sparse.*

This pattern was created in 1962 by George Biggs presently of Jerome, Idaho. It was named the Sheep Creek Special in 1970 after George demonstrated its effectiveness one afternoon by catching dozens of large trout from Sheep Creek Reservoir on the Duck Valley Indian Reservation southeast of Twin Falls.

One of its original uses was to simulate speckled dun mayfly emergers. Thus before the easy availability of sinking lines George weighted his fly to fish it near the bottom with a floating line. In this use it proved deadly in impoundments throughout southern and eastern Idaho. George relates experiences in years past when he caught trout of several pounds from impoundments in Franklin County. Now his fly is used from Iowa to California for trout, steelhead and warm water species. In sizes 2-18 it has become a versatile attractor pattern fished wet on floating and sinking lines alike. In eastern Idaho its use is popular from mountain lakes to lowland impoundments to simulate speckled dun nymphs and damselfly nymphs. In addition to demonstrated effectiveness and versatility it has the other qualities that make a fly popular; simplicity of construction from readily available materials. Its identifying features are hackle placement at the bend and a sparse mallard flank wing. The body is usually formed with olive or green chenille, but the use of black or shades of brown chenille are also popular. So is the use of grizzly, ginger, badger or hackle dyed various colors in place of the original brown.

WOOLHEAD SCULPIN

Hook: *Mustad 36890 or equivalent, sizes 2/0-4.*
Thread: *Red nylon, 2/0.*
Body: *Gold or silver sparkle braid.*
Wing: *Rabbit fur stip, olive, brown or gray.*

Pectoral Fins: *Pair of mottled pheasant flank feathers mounted with undersides forward.*
Head: *Olive rams wool clipped to shape.*

As one progresses through this section it becomes apparent that certain personalities have championed patterns into popular usage. This has been through either describing an effective presentation or making a constructive modification. Such is the case with the Woolhead Sculpin, and Doug and Mary Anne Siepert have done the most to popularize its local use.

They operate their fly tying materials business, Fur-Feather-Fly, out of Rexburg, Idaho and for years have supplied not only quality items, but also generous and constructive information on fly tying through classes, demonstrations or conversation with those who visit their business. Their flies have gained a reputation for effectiveness and durability. Such is the case with their Woolhead Sculpin which is also considered an artistic creation by many flyfishers.

The origin of the Woolhead Sculpin is obscure, most likely because of the widespread North American occurrence of Cottus species, commonly called sculpins. Cottus is a bottom dweller and is commonly found in many water types in our area, but its primary habitat is riffles and runs of freestone and gravel bottoms no more than a few feet deep. Here it is a favored food form of trout and thus imitations such as the Woolhead Sculpin should be fished close to the bottom of these water types using a sink tip line and a leader no more than two feet long. A hopping or twitching motion of the pattern as it ascends riffles and runs simulates the movements of the sculpin. The wool head is superior to a spun hollow hair head in absorbing water and this is functional in helping the fly to sink. Wool is extremely durable, thus Woolhead Sculpins last longer than those constructed with spun hollow hair heads.

WOOLLY BUGGER

Hook: *Mustad 79580 or equivalent, sizes 2-10.*
Thread: *Black monocord, 3/0.*
Tail: *Black marabou and a few pearl*
Flashabou or Krystal Flash fibers.
Body: *Black or olive chenille.*
Hackle: *Black palmered over body.*

Mid October is a beautiful time to be outdoors in eastern Idaho. Anticipating eager cutthroat or the possibility of a trophy brown, we walked through the Falls Campground in Swan Valley to fish channels on the South Fork of the Snake River one recent October day.

"You boys ain't gonna git 'cher elk with them there fly poles!" came a good natured twang from behind us.

I turned to see a middle-aged smiling face with twinkling eyes and ruddy jowls over a hunter orange vest and tan coveralls. Behind him two teenage boys carried rifles and lunches from their hunting camp to a beat up International Travel-All.

"What 'cha usin'?"

"Woolly Buggers. Ever try them here?" I answered.

"You bet 'cha! We use 'em fer hellgramites durin' the salmon fly hatch. We weight 'em with split shot and drag 'em on bottom. Got me a eight-pound German brown on one at Fall Creek Eddy back in July. Darn near broke my spinnin' pole!"

To many eastern Idaho anglers the giant stonefly nymph is known as a hellgrammite.

The use of Russ Blessing's Woolly Bugger has spread around the world from Pennsylvania in a little more than 20 years. In eastern Idaho it is definitely a favorite fly used as a streamer or even a nymph as witnessed my friend at Falls Campground a few Octobers ago. Effective as it is in streams, it is superior as a still water pattern. My experience is that it is almost indispensable for fishing beaver ponds. It can be tied to simulate leeches, damselfly nymphs, dragonfly nymphs or minnows, all of which are found in these natural impoundments. Thus it can be used all season.

TIER CREDITS

Several tiers contributed flies to be used as models for photography in this book. In many cases the contributor conceived the pattern, and thus it is appropriate that their dressing be used. I also asked other accomplished local tiers to contribute their versions of standard patterns, mainly for reasons of expedience. Almost any tier will agree that it is difficult to muster the discipline required to sit down and tie only one each of a series of patterns, and I am one of the worst at doing this. So consider the tiers in the following list to be contributors to this book and, therefore, responsible in helping it achieve any measure of success. I thank each for their contribution. I mustered enough discipline to tie the remaining patterns.

Tier	Residence	Pattern
Joe Allen	Jackson, Wyoming	Double Humpy
Troy Allgood	Teton, Idaho	Pheasant Tail Nymph
Elgarda Ashliman	Rexburg, Idaho	3 Bar X
Clayne Baker	Boise, Idaho	Prince Nymph
Dave Ball	Idaho Falls, Idaho	Joe's Hopper
Pat Barnes	Helena, Montana	Sofa Pillow
Joe Bare	Idaho Falls, Idaho	Montana Nymph
Bob Bean	Blackfoot, Idaho	Bob's Hopper
		Meat Getter
Al Beatty	Sandpoint, Idaho	Henryville Special
Jerry Berg	Soda Springs, Idaho	Sagwah
		Whiskey Creek
Glen Bitton	Pocatello, Idaho	Bitton Special
Phil Blomquist	Pocatello, Idaho	Phil's Hopper
Paul Bowen	Rexburg, Idaho	EZ Hopper
		Pale Morning Dun
Steve Christensen	Ririe, Idaho	LC Moose
Chuck Collins	Pocatello, Idaho	Gray Wulff
		Royal Wulff
Floyd Fantelli	Idaho Falls, Idaho	Hornberg
Bill Fuger	Idaho Falls, Idaho	Velour Stonefly Nymph
		Yellow Sally
Jim Gabettas	Idaho Falls, Idaho	Carmichael
Jimmy Gabettas	Pocatello, Idaho	Humpy
Buck Goodrich	Shelley, Idaho	Muddler Minnow
Hazel Hansen	Overton, Nevada	Teton Queen
Bonnie Harrop	St. Anthony, Idaho	Speckled Biot Spinner
Rene Harrop	St. Anthony, Idaho	Hair Wing Dun
Ruth Harrop	Rexburg, Idaho	Elk Hair Caddis
Marv Hoyt	Idaho Falls, Idaho	Soft Hackled Fly
Bob Jacklin	West Yellowstone, Montana	March Brown Nymph
Neil Komoda	Idaho Falls, Idaho	Neil's Stonefly
Joe Kortum, Sr. (deceased)	Pocatello, Idaho	Lady Mite
Jim Lambert	Rexburg, Idaho	Super Renegade
Mike Lawson	St. Anthony, Idaho	Spent Partridge Caddis
Bing Lempke (deceased)	Idaho Falls, Idaho	Bing's Hopper
		Blue Winged Olive
		Green Drake
Craig Mathews	West Yellowstone, Montana	Blue Ribbon Beetle
Ralph Moon	Chester, Idaho	Mormon Girl
Scott Moss	Idaho Falls, Idaho	Moss Caddis Emerger
		Moss Stonefly

Tier	Residence	Pattern
Wes Newman	Idaho Falls, Idaho	Rag Wing Dun
Marcella Oswald	Idaho Falls, Idaho	Marcella's Troutfly
Fred Petersen	Idaho Falls, Idaho	Mickey Finn
Kathy Radford	Ririe, Idaho	Boyle's Shrimp
Kevin Radford	Ririe, Idaho	Fizzler
Becky Robbins	Pingree, Idaho	Gray Hackle Peacock
Doug Siepert	Rexburg, Idaho	Woolhead Sculpin
Mary Anne Siepert	Rexburg, Idaho	Goddard Caddis
Cliff Stringer	Nampa, Idaho	North Fork Fly
Dennis Swanson	Idaho Falls, Idaho	Gold Ribbed Hare's Ear
Bob Trowbridge	Providence, Utah	Adams
Pete Wiswell	Jackson, Wyoming	Bitch Creek Nymph
		Marabou Muddler

Spring ponds such as these garland the Snake River Plain adjacent to the north side of American Falls Reservoir. Rainbow, cutthroat and hybrid trout prosper in these ponds, and a number of them have become trout farms to supply culinary demands around the world. Bruce Staples

BIBLIOGRAPHY

Boone, Lalia.; *Idaho Place Names, A Geographical Dictionary*, The University of Idaho Press, Moscow, Idaho, 1988.

Brooks, Charles E.; *The Henry's Fork*, Nick Lyons Books, New York, New York, 1986.

Brooks, Charles E.; *Nymph Fishing for Larger Trout*, Crown Publishers, Inc., New York, New York, 1976.

Brosnam, Cornelius J.; *History of the State of Idaho*, Charles Scribner's Sons, New York, New York, 1935.

Dennis, Jack; *Western Trout Fly Tying Manual*, Volume I, Snake River Books, Jackson Hole, Wyoming, 1974.

Dennis, Jack; *Western Trout Fly Tying Manual*, Volume II, Snake River Books, Jackson Hole, Wyoming, 1980.

Driggs, B. W.; *History of Teton Valley*, edited by L. J. Clements and H. S. Forbush, Eastern Idaho Publishing Co., Rexburg, Idaho, 1970.

Goddard, John; *Trout Flies on Still Water*, Adam, Charles and Black, London, U. K. 1979.

Grant, George F.; *Montana Trout Flies*, Champoeg Press, Portland, Oregon, 1981.

Haddock, Edith P. and Mathews, Dorothy H.; *History of the Bear Lake Pioneers*, Daughters of the Utah Pioneers, Bear Lake County Idaho, 1968.

Hafele, Rick and Hughes, Dave: *Western Hatches*, Frank Amato Publications, Portland Oregon, 1981.

Hellekson, Terry; *Popular Fly Pattern*, Peregrine Smith Inc., Salt Lake City, Utah, 1977.

Irving, J. S., Elle, F. S. and Bjornn, T. C.; *The Fish Populations and Fishery in the Teton River Prior to Impoundment by Teton Dam*, Forest, Wildlife, and Range Experiment Station, University of Idaho, 1977.

Jeppson, Paul; *Management of the Henry's Fork Fishery*, Idaho Department of Fish and Game, unpublished, 1978.

Lovell, Edith H.; *Captain Bonneville's County*, The Eastern Idaho Farmer, Idaho Falls, Idaho, 1963.

MacDonald, Alexander; *On Becoming a Fly Fisherman*, David McKay Co., New York, New York, 1959.

Maley, Terry; *Exploring Idaho Geology*, Mineral Lands Publications, Boise, Idaho, 1987.

Marbury, Mary O.; *Favorite Flies and Their Histories*, The Wellfleet Press, Secaucus, New Jersey, 1988.

Martin, Darrel; *Fly-Tying Methods*, Nick Lyons Books, New York, New York, 1987.

Mathews, Craig and Juracek, John; *Fly Patterns of Yellowstone*, Blue Ribbon Flies, West Yellowstone, Montana, 1987.

McCarthy, Max R.; *The Last Chance Canal Company*, The Charles Redd Center for Western Studies, Brigham Young University, Provo, Utah, 1987.

Nemes, Sylvester; *The Soft-Hackled Fly*, The Chatham Press, Old Greenwich, Connecticut, 1975.

Nemes, Sylvester; *The Soft-Hackled Fly Addict*, Published by the Author, Chicago, Illinois, 1981.

Perrault, Keith E.; *Perrault's Standard Dictionary of Fishing Flies*, Kepcor, Orlando, Florida, 1984.

Rhodenbaugh, Edward F.; *Sketches of Idaho Geology*, Caxton Printers, Caldwell, Idaho, 1953.

Rockwell, Irvin E.; *The Saga of American Falls Dam*, The Hobson Book Press, New York, New York, 1947.

Sawyer, Frank; *Nymphs and the Trout*, Stanley Paul and Co., Ltd, London, U. K., 1958.

Schullery, Paul; *American Fly Fishing*, Nick Lyons Books, New York, New York, 1986.

Schwiebert, Ernest; *Trout*, E. P. Dutton, New York, New York, 1978.

Shupe, Irene; *Caribou City Chronology*, Printcraft Press, Colorado Springs, Colorado, 1930.

Palisades Creek is the largest tributary to the reach of the Snake River that east Idahoans call the South Fork. Flowing southwesterly out of the Snake River Range to meet the South Fork, it is a spawning stream of major importance for the Snake River fine spotted cutthroat. Its setting is also among the most beautiful of any eastern Idaho stream. Bruce Staples

Along the Trail Creek Road and into Copper Basin, Big Lost River and its tributaries provide quality rainbow and brook trout fishing. Catch and release regulations have been applied to portions of this drainage, and good numbers of trophy rainbow trout could result. Dennis Bitton

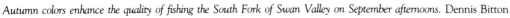

Autumn colors enhance the quality of fishing the South Fork of Swan Valley on September afternoons. Dennis Bitton

INDEX

Meadow Creek; 43, 46
Medicine Lodge Creek; 52
Menan Buttes; 11, 14, 24, 51
Mesa Falls Scenic Loop; 30
McCoy Creek; 37, 66
McCoy, Mike; 5
McCue, Jim; 5
McKinney, Bear; 5
McTucker Creek; 12
Michigan; 21, 62, 64
Michigan Hopper; 73
Mickey Finn; 87
Midge; 21
Mill Creek; 53
Mill Creek Lake; 53
Mink Creek; 50
Missoula, Montana; 77
Mite Series; 76, 77
Monida Pass; 51
Montana; 6, 21, 62, 69, 71, 77, 79, 83, 86
Montana Black Nymph; 82, 85
Monterey, California; 84
Montpelier Creek; 50
Moon, Ralph; 5, 69
Moose Creek; 22
Moose Lake; 54
Moose, Wyoming; 65, 67, 78
Mormon Girl; 61, 69, 71
Moss Caddis Emerger; 83
Moss, Scott; 83
Moss Stonefly Nymph; 83
Mountain Ash Creek; 32
Mount Borah; 54
Muddler Minnow; 58, 87, 88
Mud Lake; 51, 52
Muskrat Nymph; 82

N5 Ranch; 78
Neil's Stonefly; 70
Nemes, Sylvester; 78
New Jersey; 82
Newman, Wes; 67, 76, 78
New York; 21, 59, 65, 82
New York City; 61
New Zealand; 87
Nipigon River; 87
Noback; 77
North American Waters; 67, 84, 88
North Fork Fly; 60
North Fork of the Big Lost River; 54
North Fork of the Teton River; 14

Ogden, Utah; 80
Ohio; 64
Olive Dun; 21
Oneida County; 10, 50
Oneida Dam; 10
Oneida Reservoir; 50
Ontario, Canada; 87
Oregon Trail; 10, 13
Ormond, Clyde; 82
Osborne Bridge; 19
Oswald, Harvey; 69
Oswald, Marcella; 69

Pacific Coast; 61, 67
Pacific Ocean; 47
Pale Morning Dun; 21, 67
Palisades Creek; 37
Palisades Dam; 11, 24-26, 37, 75, 87
Palisades Lakes; 37
Palisades Reservoir; 24, 28, 37, 38
Parachute Pale Morning Dun; 67
Partridge Creek; 30
Pat Barnes Tackle Shop; 70
Peacock Adams; 64
Peale Range; 38, 44

Pebble Creek; 47, 48
Pennsylvania; 21, 79, 89
Petersen, Fred; 58
Pheasant Tail Nymph; 79, 84
Phil's Hopper; 74
Picket Pin; 71
Pine Creek; 37
Pinedale, Wyoming; 74
Pinehaven Village; 17
Pioneer Range; 51, 53, 54
Pitchstone Plateau; 32
Pocatello, Idaho; 74, 77
Poplar, Idaho; 25
Porcupine Creek; 31
Portneuf Canyon; 47
Portneuf Range; 47,
Portneuf River; 10, 11,47, 48, 79
Portneuf Valley; 47
Pott, Franz; 76, 77
Preuss Creek; 50
Preuss Range; 49
Prince, Doug; 84
Prince Nymph; 84
Pritchard Creek; 37
Professor; 60
Provo River; 69

Quill Cahill; 66

Rainey Creek; 37
Radford, Etsel; 76
Radford, Kathy; 75, 76
Radford, Kevin; 75, 76
Rag Wing Duns; 67
Railroad Ranch; 19 59
Rassumussen Ridge; 44
Rat Faced McDougal; 60
Red Road; 51
Red Rock Pass; 47
Renegade; 60, 61, 77, 78
Reverse Renegade; 61
Rexburg, Idaho; 15, 69, 84, 88
Rio Grande Trude; 71
Ririe, Idaho; 66, 75, 76, 78,
Ririe Dam; 11
Ririe Reservoir; 40
Riverside Campground; 14, 15, 17
Roberts, Harold; 5
Robinson Creek; 16, 30, 31, 66
Rock Creek; 31
Rocky Mountains; 61, 69
Roscoe, New York; 60
Royal Coachman; 54, 61, 69
Royal Coachman Streamer; 61
Royal Renegade; 54, 61
Royal Trude; 61, 71
Royal Wulff; 60, 61
Rubber Legs; 81

Sage Creek; 38
Sagwah; 77
Saint Anthony, Idaho; 21, 63, 66, 68, 83
Saint Charles Creek; 50
Salt River; 24, 38, 39, 47, 65, 79, 86
Salt River Range; 24
Salmon River; 51, 53, 54, 75
Sandy Mite; 76, 77
San Francisco, California; 68
Sawmill Creek; 53
Sawyer, Frank; 84
Schiess, Bill; 8, 75
Scotland; 61
Scully, Dick; 5
Sevier River; 10
Sheep Creek Reservoir; 88
Sheep Creek Special; 88
Sheep Falls, Falls River; 32

Sheep Falls, Henry's Fork; 17
Sheepskin Road; 13
Shelley, Idaho; 86
Sheridan Creek; 22
Shindurling, Ace; 77
Shoshone Falls; 11
Shotgun Creek; 22
Siepert, Doug; 88
Siepert, Mary Anne; 88
Silver Creek; 28, 55
Slate Cream Dun; 21
Slate Wing Olive; 21
Slough Creek; 44
Small, Idaho (Medicine Lodge, Idaho); 51
Snake River; 10-14, 24, 47, 51, 86
Snake River Plain; 10, 11, 26, 29, 32, 45, 47, 51, 52, 54, 55, 73
Snake River Range; 24, 37
Soda Point Dam; 10
Soda Springs, Idaho; 77, 79
Sofa Pillow; 60, 68, 70, 71
Soft Hackled Fly; 77, 78
South Fork Lodge; 78
South Fork of the Snake River; 10-12, 15, 24-28, 34, 59, 64-69, 71, 73-76, 78-80, 86, 89
South Fork Road; 25
South Fork Tributaries; 37
Speckled Biot Spinner; 67
Speckled Dun; 21
Spencer, Idaho; 51
Spent Partridge Caddis; 63, 64, 69
Springfield Reservoir; 12, 13
Spring Creek, Little; 38
Spring Creek, Salt River Drainage; 38
Spring Creek, Snake River Drainage; 12
Spuddler; 88
Squirrel Creek; 33, 77
Stan's Flies; 62, 74
Stan's Hopper; 74
Stan's Willow Fly; 70, 71
Staples, Barry; 5
Staples, Carol; 5
Starhope Creek; 54
Star Valley; 38
State Highway 28; 53
State Highway 31; 37
State Highway 34; 58
Stiff; 79
Stiffie; 79
Stocking Family; 44
Stump Creek; 38, 39, 65
Sugar City, Idaho; 21
Summit Creek; 53
Sun Valley, Idaho; 28, 61
Super Renegade; 61, 78
Super X; 78
Surprise Falls; 17
Swan Lake, Idaho; 47
Swan Valley, Idaho; 10, 24-26, 37, 74, 78, 89
Swanson, Dennis; 79
Swauger Lakes; 53

Teton Canyon; 10, 34
Teton County; 80
Teton Dam; 11, 14, 34, 84
Teton Valley Fly Shop; 78
Tetonia; 78
Teton King; 78, 79
Teton Queen; 78, 79
Teton Range; 24, 32, 36, 65
Teton River; 34-36, 47, 67, 69, 78, 85
Teton Valley; 10, 36, 65, 78, 80
The Fingers; 22
The Meat Getter; 64
The Tubs; 22
Thomas Fork; 49
Thousand Springs Valley; 54, 55

Following page: *With a steep gradient Falls River leaves the southwest corner of Yellowstone National Park and courses through Freemont County to meet the Henry's Fork just above the Chester irrigation diversion. Prized by white water enthusiasts and anglers alike the upper reach of the Falls River is eastern Idaho's most unspoiled larger river. Bruce Staples*